Halo Again

A JOURNEY IN

COMMUNICATION INTELLIGENCE

For Life-Long Relationships

Paul V. Spampanato

www.haloagain.com

i

Author: Paul V. Spampanato
Cover Design: Nina Walters & Paul V. Spampanato
Prepared for Publication by: Elizabeth Wirth

ISBN-13: 978-1480049901
ISBN-10: 1480049905

Cataloging-in-Publication Data
Spampanato, Paul V.
Halo again : a journey in communication intelligence for life long relationships / Paul V. Spampanato.
xiii, 205 p. : b ill. ; 23 cm.
ISBN 978-1-480-04990-1 (pbk.)

1. Man-woman relationships. 2. Communication in marriage.
3. Interpersonal communication 4. Interpersonal relations.
I. Title

HQ734

First printing 2012
Second printing 2014

Dedication

To my father, mother, and sister, Giovanna, for their unconditional love and support. Also, thanks to all my students and the many friends who nurtured, shared, encouraged, and showed me that you can achieve any goal if you never stop working toward it.

"Time and reflection change the sight little by little 'til we come to understand."

Paul Cezanne

CONTENTS

INTRODUCTION

"We do not exist for ourselves."

Thomas Merton

-Introduction-

Throughout our lives, most often by chance, we all have experiences that teach us about ourselves or change the direction we are heading. While we gain perspective from these experiences, we often fail to see the greater relevance that they bring to us, because there is usually more than one lesson to be learned from any experience.

About eight years ago, while living in Rochester, NY, I went to the Spencerport Public Library with my children. Outside, the library had boxes of books they were disposing of on sale for five cents each. Since I love books I naturally began to look through them for anything my family and I might enjoy. Curiously enough I found a book that looked really old with its binding coming apart and wondered if it had any value. The book, *Plutarch*, was a compilation of stories titled *Lives of Illustrious Men*. Having been a student of philosophy, and being of Italian descent, I pored through the pages, specifically taking in the tales of a number of Roman Generals: Caesar, Marcellus, Pompey, Camillus and others.

Several months after I made this extravagant purchase, a good friend, who had once lived in Syracuse, invited me to spend the day fishing with him near there. On the drive over, as we neared our destination, I saw a sign for Camillus, NY, which, as it turned out, is where my friend told me he was originally from. Excited by hearing this, I began telling him the story of the great Roman General Camillus. Camillus had been a great soldier, but as politics often play out, he was impeached by his adversaries and opted for exile rather than paying fines falsely levied upon him. Later while still in exile, he, along with others, saved Rome from the invading Gauls, becoming a hero to Rome once again. After listening to the lengthy tale with interest, my friend declared that I should be a teacher. A little over three years later, I began teaching. One little nickel led me to a career that I had not chosen earlier, but was in me all along. I didn't see it myself until someone else saw the enthusiasm I had for sharing what I had learned, and pointed out the value that book had for me. That nickel changed my life.

Later, I began to share this story with my *Success Strategies* students, to demonstrate that interdependence can take you to places you might not have thought you could go. The very first time I shared the story of my nickel with a class I asked them, "Do you believe that a nickel can change your life?" One of my students replied, "Not likely, unless you have an ocean of them." His perception was, as most of the students in the class I believe, that nothing so small, that has so little value, can really make a difference. Purchasing that book alone might not have led me to become a teacher. It was sharing what I read with someone else and his positive feedback, that interdependence that changed my life. The story, however, didn't end there.

A year ago I received a teaching award from the community college where I am an instructor. One is typically nominated for this award by their peers. In this case, however, I had been nominated by a student who had benefited from the story I had shared with the class. One who found her life changed, similarly, by another nickel! In the letter she sent an administrator at the college, she shared that one evening, as she was leaving the restaurant where she worked, she saw a customer drop a piece of change on the floor. Bending down to pick the coin up, she laughed to herself when she discovered that it was a nickel. She called out to the customer, "Sir, I saved your nickel. You may really need this one day!" The man gave her a funny look and said, "It's just a nickel." "Sir, this nickel may just change your life one day." she said, and began to tell him about the story of the nickel that I shared with my students. During the conversation she noticed that he was wearing a shirt that had *Virginia* on it. She then shared that she was going there soon to spend some time visiting four colleges. She planned to study to become a Doctor of Radiology. It turns out that he was an alumnus of one of the colleges she was interested in, as well as a doctor himself, teaching at one of the other colleges. He was so impressed that he offered to help her, in any way that he could, to obtain a scholarship and possibly an internship as a radiologist. Stunned, she realized that his nickel was changing her life! Tell me now that a nickel has no real value!

We've all heard the expressions, *"Putting in my two cents worth,"* or *"A penny for your thoughts,"* and now, as I've learned and shared, five cents can be all it takes to change your life! If small change can create bigger change, then why don't we apply this concept in our most intimate relationships? What I am trying to impress here, is that we tend to take so much for granted in our lives, especially involving those closest to us. We often do not place the same value on our personal lives as we do on our other successes. What is worse, we do not place enough value on each other in our relationships. There was truly so much more to be gained from those five cents. The lesson I learned from that simple five cent purchase was what I failed to discover in my marriage until it was too late. In my relationship, my wife and I lacked the interdependence that I gained from my friend. I didn't share with, or receive from my wife, similar encouragement.

I've written this book to show you what I've discovered from my own life experience, to help you, throughout this book and culminating in the final chapter, see the real value in interdependence -- how important it is to the success of any relationship.

CHAPTER ONE

Communication Intelligence &

The Communication Compass

**"The "four winds of success" now blow
to me my own. From North, South, East
and West comes my endless good."**
Florence Scovel Shinn

- Chapter One -

I never realized, until I began writing this book, how many relationship experts there are in the world. If so many people know how to make relationships succeed, then why do so many relationships still fail? Why do statistics indicate that over 50% of marriages end in divorce? Isn't there already enough information out there to ensure our happiness if we just follow a few simple steps? Simple, they call them, as if they were writing an instruction manual to assemble a time travel machine out of a De Lorean.

Relationships, though, are anything but simple. They are an intricate puzzle comprised of interwoven fragments of the emotions, logic, expectations, and dreams of two individuals. There is no clear pattern in the pieces and there is no single right way to put it all together. As anyone who has ever assembled a puzzle knows, most find it is easy to work from the outside in, building the edges first. Others, however, work best by looking for common colors and putting together recognizable images such as trees, animals or buildings first.

I have seen, through experience, a direct correlation between relationships and puzzles based on how we choose to assemble them. This involves the dichotomy between *Expectation* and *Expectancy*. I began to see that, much like the majority of us who begin a puzzle by putting together the edges first, we have an expectation that this is the easiest route. We establish a boundary based on the expectation that all the internal pieces will then fall easily into place, believing that the puzzle only has meaning when the pieces are seen as part of a whole.

In contrast, those who assemble recognizable shapes first have the expectancy that even if the puzzle is never finished, or is missing pieces, there are still some beautiful elements to be displayed and appreciated. Expectancy differs from expectation in that expectancy allows you to see the silver lining -- the good that comes from any situation, even when it does not turn out as planned. In essence, expectancy allows us to accept that relationships are never perfect, and that not all of the "pieces" we "expect" to be there are necessary for us to be happy in them.

**"Life can only be understood backwards,
but it must be lived forwards."**
Soren Kierkegaard

For years, as a communication instructor, I have both studied and taught Emotional Intelligence and its contribution to successful Conflict Management in relationships. Emotional Intelligence, well established since its introduction in the early 1990's, and sound in its principles, primarily deals with learning how to harness one's emotions based on conditions imposed on us by others. That is, how to deliver appropriate encouragement (through leadership and teamwork) and appropriate responses (through conflict management) based on an *expectation* of the outcome. I do not disagree with the basic principles of Emotional Intelligence, but I do believe that Communication Intelligence -- adapting to the same conditions that create conflict with a mindset of *expectancy* -- will serve to broaden one's perspective and allow for more effective communication.

I began to theorize that much like putting together the border of a puzzle first, by only learning to control our emotions we are still setting boundaries, or certain expectations, for our relationships. Communication Intelligence, then, is the ability to set aside the constraints that expectations place on our relationships, and to replace them with expectancy. I propose that Communication Intelligence, while not intended to replace Emotional Intelligence, will serve to enhance its foundation. It does this by offering us another instrument that we can use to achieve success in our relationships. Expectancy gives us the ability to seek out what is good about our relationships, instead of allowing dissatisfaction to set in when expectations are not being met. As a result, you are able to create a much more positive communication climate!

Expectations generally limit our behavior, because expectations are typically rooted in our beliefs and are often false assumptions. Consequently, expectations have a profound influence on how we communicate with each other and most often lead to negative feelings. Expectancy, unlike expectation, is not a predetermined belief, but rather a *hope* that with encouragement becomes something positive. It is possible to believe in a negative outcome, but when was the last time you hoped for one? Expectations are generally predetermined, if not by us then for us, causing us to focus more on what we believe defines us, rather than on our potential. As I will share with you throughout this book, expectancy will not only guide you to more effective communication, it will also open your heart and mind to the willingness to nurture, encourage, share, and work together in a relationship. Really, how simple is that?

Ok, by now you are asking yourself, "Where is this guy coming from?" I am a man, with a Master's Degree in Communication, who recently exited a marriage of twenty years without having one intelligible conversation with my wife during the last two years. I am not a psychologist, nor a marriage counselor, nor a relationship expert. How does one, exactly, become an expert on something so ever-changing and complex? I imagine that you are thinking that I have nothing new to offer. If you allow me, however, to take you through my voyage of discovery I can assure you that I get it now! While the way we communicate with each other is based on the value we place on each other, without action, without demonstrating to your partner how important they are to you, that value is simply another expectation.

The words I love you are easily said, but are meaningless if our actions do not support what we say. Communication Intelligence, the combination of words and actions, give us hope for a bright and lasting future through nurturing, encouraging, sharing and above all, working together to achieve that lasting goal. I have come to learn that I placed more value on what I expected than on what I hoped for. It is a common statement that you attract what you put out there, so your actions in a relationship are as important as your words. To achieve the value you are looking for in your relationship, you must treat your partner as if they are that "one in a million." When you begin to understand how to attract the right person in your life, in terms of relationships you become a millionaire!

While all relationships encounter detours at some point, it is our failure to heed the warning signs, our reluctance to put any effort into restoring what we feel we have lost, and our misconception that people are as easy to replace as objects, that ultimately cause most relationship failures. This pattern of denial is often the result of ineffective communication between our self and our partner and it revolves in large part around unmet expectations we set in the beginning for our partner and for the relationship.

Some of the earliest warning signs of a relationship failure can be as simple as noticing little habits that never bothered you about your partner before, or vice versa. Consequently, these things often become reasons for conflict and not communication. It can literally be as simple as getting annoyed with which way your partner places the toilet paper on the holder…roll over, roll under. Cliché, I know, but it is these seemingly inconsequential annoyances that encourage our belief (expectation) that the relationship will ultimately fail.

"Almost all of our relationships begin and most of them continue as forms of mutual exploitation, a mental or physical barter, to be terminated when one or both parties run out of goods."
W.H. Auden

When relationships lose momentum due to lack of direction, we find ourselves arguing instead of communicating, much as we do on a trip when we take a wrong turn and find ourselves lost. We are afraid to stop and admit to our self and our partner that we are lost. We are afraid to ask for directions. This reluctance can delay or cancel our journey altogether. Despite all the clinical textbook definitions of communication, it is, simply, the most basic form of human interaction. If you don't learn to communicate effectively, your relationship can get so far off course that steering it back in a positive direction may seem impossible.

"While we are postponing, life speeds by."
Lucius Annaeus Seneca

Of all the lessons we learn in life, those we learn as children exert the most profound influence. The beauty of childhood is that our minds are innocent, uncluttered, and without prejudice. Unfortunately, this innocence wanes as we are acculturated into society by our families, friends, neighbors and teachers. These influences strongly contribute to the opinions, behaviors, and expectations we form regarding how we are to treat people. Not just our friends and neighbors, but family members and the one with whom we will form our most intimate relationship.

I am a first-generation Italian-American. My parents emigrated from Italy after World War II. My expectations of love and relationships were like those of my parents and older relatives, because that was what I saw around me as I was growing up. Emulation of what we see is natural, especially if we are very young when we first set sail on that life-long journey that is marriage, as I did and as so many people do. Remember, our parents were raised in a different time and place. Men and women had specific role assignments and happiness was secondary to the fulfillment of those roles. Duty prevailed.

Our American culture, especially today, is based more on individualism than obligation and roles. As long as we hold on exclusively to the old ways, we find it harder to adapt. I am not saying that the lessons our parents were taught and passed on to us were wrong, rather, as with education and technology, there is always something new to learn. Ironically, I have discovered that while we believe individualism differentiates us from those established cultural and generational norms, individualism is equally rooted in expectation. It doesn't matter whether we know what we want (individualism) or we know what we are expected to be (norm), both are subjective to a presupposed outcome. In either case we set limits and close our minds to growth and opportunity feeling there is neither nothing new to learn, nor to hope for. It is through learning that we grow as people. Learning is a form of expectancy, but knowledge alone is powerless without action. To take action -- to live our lives with expectancy -- we need to be willing to open our minds, as we did as children, in order to truly discover who we may become.

My voyage of life and love began over twenty years ago with my high school sweetheart. While I loved her, as much as any teenager can comprehend love at that age, I believe the expectations we set for each other ultimately broke the bond we believed could not be broken. It wasn't until after that bond was irrevocably broken that my eyes were opened to a striking reality: more often than not in relationships, we do not truly value each other until after a loss. The most interesting discovery I've made from my experience, is that we wait until we really need each other to tell each other how much we need each other! Far too often, we wait too long and we lose. It should *never* take loss for anyone to realize how precious our lives and our relationships are. We need to cherish every moment of our lives together, because these, be they few or many, are the only moments we will have.

"Treasure each other in the recognition that we do not know how long we shall have each other."
Joshua L. Liebman

Why *Halo Again*? By now I'm sure you are wondering how that relates to Communication Intelligence. I, as well as nearly everyone who enters a relationship, regardless of the circumstance, have succumbed to the Halo Effect. The Halo Effect is currently described as a psychological bias based on the expectation that *"what is physically beautiful is good."*

First identified in 1920 by Edward L. Thorndike, an American psychologist and theorist, he described the Halo Effect as a "constant error." In his study of the ratings of Army officers, provided by their superiors, he noted erroneous correlations in the scores. The study asked for individual ratings based on physique, intelligence, leadership, and character. Thorndike discovered that a perception based on one particular feature created unrealistic correlations, a generalization, of all other ratings. For example, if the officer was physically attractive, it might then be assumed that he was a strong leader, intelligent, and possessed strong character. The ratings reflected this accordingly. Thorndike concluded, "This same constant error toward suffusing [flooding] ratings of special features with a halo belonging to the individual as a whole appeared in the ratings of officers made by their superiors in the army." Simply put, he discovered that what you see is not necessarily what you get.

The most innocent account of the Halo Effect was, for me, as a child -- an open-minded, unprejudiced child. While attending St. Charles Borromeo School in Rochester, NY, I remember going with my class to the school library to pick out a book. From a very young age I have loved to read and I immediately sat down to turn the pages of my chosen book. To my surprise, inside my book was a picture of a young black girl in a cute school dress leaning towards a fountain with a sign over it that read "colored." Excited by this, imagining fountains of colored water flowing like liquid rainbows, I ran with the book to my teacher and eagerly asked her, "Why don't we have colored fountains here?" I remember the look on her face, and I remember that the answer the teacher gave me both confused and saddened me. What appeared to me to be something wonderfully sweet and exciting was, in reality, a horrible depiction of a group of people *not* dissimilar from anyone else. The little girl was, after all, just a child like me. That moment of realization that ugliness in life is often hidden behind beauty, and that baseless expectations are set by society for those who are different has not only remained with me to this day, but it has defined me as a person. Later, this experience contributed to shaping me as a teacher.

"I threw my cup away when I saw a child drinking from his hands at the trough."
Diogenes

That childhood experience has shown me that expectations are often the Halo Effects judgmental bias and that expectations limit what we are willing to see and communicate. Expectancy allows you to focus on describing how you honestly feel. Moreover, it allows you to focus on the unique qualities you both have, and to identify what you are hoping for in your relationship. By looking at your relationship as an opportunity to grow, instead of an obligation to maintain, you can look outside the cultural and situational constraints that expectations place on you. *Halo Again*, allows you to search for those opportunities for growth that exist in all of us, instead of constantly searching for perfection based on unrealistic expectations. The key here then is to learn how to harness and use communication more effectively, more intelligently.

Thorndike's initial theory, and the many others that have followed, have demonstrated over and over that the Halo Effect is an instinctive reaction. The Halo Effect is something we all experience, in some way or another, as early as childhood. It affects nearly every aspect of our lives, but is most pronounced in our close personal relationships. This is because we tend to set expectations based on what we first see. We do not evaluate the whole picture. In our everyday lives, we look around us for physical beauty, and for most of us, this is what we first form our relationships on. We never assume that something beautiful on the outside could be ugly on the inside, or conversely, that something not so attractive on the outside could, in fact, be beautiful on the inside.

In business, especially, we often predict the value of a potential employee based on what he or she looks like rather than the skills he or she possesses. In other words, we set expectations of people based primarily on outward appearances, the facades, instead of what we hope they have to offer. Suffice it to say, it is a poor determining factor of someone's true worth or potential because, as with treasure, most beauty is hidden and waiting to be discovered. The expectations we set, based on what we believe we see, often lead to failure in our relationships. *Halo Again* seeks to counter the Halo Effect using expectancy, allowing us to see the potential in a relationship, instead of succumbing to a predetermined expectation based on a single initial impression.

The Halo Effect, or "constant error" as defined by Thorndike, is the result of using only our sight to find love, beauty, and character. *Halo Again* asks you not only to consider what drives what you choose to see – but, also, teaches you to look deeper, not just in others but in yourself. In this way, *Halo Again* enables you to use your eyes to see the potential in others, your lips to encourage them to grow, and your heart to help others realize how valuable they are. *Halo Again* inspires the willingness to hold out your hands to others to show them they are never alone. Through expectancy, you can understand that people are not just objects, and that each of us possesses unique gifts that help shape our world as well as our relationships.

The objective, then, of *Halo Again* is to not only help you find love if you haven't, but to continue to grow it if you already have. To love, and be loved, we must embark on a voyage of discovery together. My goal is to help you see how very simple it is to find it together. Remember, we are not loved because we are beautiful; we are beautiful because we are loved! To do this we need to look inside for the inner child we may have lost along the way, to allow us to see the true beauty in everything, as we did as children.

> **"If we could all see the world through the eyes of a child, we would see the magic in everything."**
> *Chee Vai Tang*

Far too often, when things begin to go badly for us, especially in relationships, we go into a sort of survival mode. This does not work to maintain, or mend, a relationship because the term survival implies that one person is in peril; each man for his self so to speak. We just need to allow ourselves to return to that time in our life when we were unbiased, unprejudiced, and most importantly, unafraid.

Halo Again, my philosophy on relationship communication, is based on a new model of Communication Intelligence guided by a compass. This model shows that if we replace our expectations with expectancy, we can change the direction of our relationship as often as we need to. If one has become disillusioned in a relationship, if the halo we placed over it has lost its glow, restoration is possible! We must allow ourselves to see, and communicate to each other often, the good we see in each other.

> **"The good is the beautiful."**
> *Plato*

I realized much too late that I never allowed myself to see or even explore the depths of who my wife truly was. Instead, from the beginning I arbitrarily placed that halo above her, setting unrealistic expectations of her in the process. We certainly all know that none of us is perfect, yet we still continue to seek perfection in others.

It is an enormous burden we place on our relationships. Near the end of my relationship, I felt betrayed by my wife, based on those expectations I had set for her, and for our relationship. As she pulled away from me, instead of communicating my feelings to her, hoping for a different outcome, I simply served her with divorce papers. I did this believing that my relationship had failed, and could not be restored. I later came to realize, that in the twenty years we were together, it was our expectations of each other that failed to allow us, or the relationship, to grow.

Over these last two years, I've done both external and internal analyses of my situation. I discovered that while I possessed all the necessary tools, to either preserve my relationship or, at the very least, part more amicably, I didn't act upon the one primary aspect of communication: the two-way process. Only through communication can we continue on our voyage of discovery, of learning ancw about each other, to keep the relationship growing. Failing to, or refusing to communicate with each other only leads to regret.

"Nothing haunts us like the things we don't say."
Mitch Albom

Probably the greatest influence on my life, learning, and ultimately the conclusions I arrived at in this book came from the "Lesson from the Geese," originally written in 1972 by Dr. Robert McNeish of Baltimore, and referenced in a newspaper article I read in the Rochester, NY *Democrat and Chronicle* while I was in graduate school. *"Lesson"* has been widely adapted and referenced by numerous authors, lecturers, and instructors throughout the years, serving as a valuable tool in explaining, most commonly to business people, the characteristics of migrating geese and how these characteristics apply to the concept of teamwork, of working together towards a united goal. There is much to be drawn from this article, and over the last five years that I have been teaching, I began to see that the employment of these lessons not only applied to large groups of individuals, but the same principles were just as applicable in our close personal relationships as well, that team of two.

Lesson From The Geese

In the fall when you see geese heading south for the winter flying along in a "V" formation, you might be interested in knowing what science has discovered about why they fly that way. There is an interdependence in the way geese function.

Fact: As each bird flaps its wings it creates an uplift for the bird immediately following. By flying in a "V" formation, the whole flock adds at least 71% greater flying range than if each bird flew on its own.

Lesson: People who share a common direction and sense of community can get where they are going quicker and easier because they are traveling on the thrust of one another.

Fact: Whenever a goose falls out of formation, it suddenly feels the drag and resistance of trying to go it alone and quickly gets back into formation to take advantage of the lifting power of the bird immediately in front.

Lesson: There is strength and power and safety in numbers when traveling in the same direction with those with whom we share a common goal. If we have as much sense as a goose, we will stay in formation with those who are headed where we want to go.

Fact: When the lead goose gets tired, he rotates back in the wing and another goose flies point.

Lesson: It pays to take turns doing hard jobs and sharing leadership—people, as with geese, are interdependent with each other.

Fact: The geese honk from behind to encourage those up front to keep up their speed.

Lesson: We all need to be remembered with active support and praise. We need to make sure our "honking" from behind is encouraging, not something less helpful.

Fact: When a goose gets sick or wounded and falls out, two geese fall out of formation and follow him down to help and protect him. They stay with him until the crisis resolves, and then they launch out on their own or with another formation to catch up with their group.

Lesson: We must stand by each other in times of need. If we have as much sense as the geese, we will.

By Dr. Robert MacNeish, Associate Superintendent of Baltimore Public Schools. Baltimore, MD. 1972.

After discovering how expectations limit our choices and direction, realizing how expectancy allows us to change and grow, understanding the impact of the Halo Effect, and incorporating the valuable lessons we learned from the geese, I began to develop *Halo Again*. I sought to apply all of these concepts to how we should interact with each other to promote more effective communication; the result was a communication compass.

Every compass has four principal orientations, *N S E W*, also known as the cardinal points. The four orientations of the Communication Compass are similar in that each cardinal point denotes a primary direction in your relationship. Much like navigating, while you are heading only one direction at a time, all of the other points allow you to get your bearing straight. To properly use a compass, you must first identify the direction you need to be going. This depends on where you are, or where you want to be, in your relationship. All other points on the compass serve as a point of reference. How would you know if you were traveling North if there were no South, East, or West points? With no bearings, it would be easy to lose your way. You would be unable to determine your position in relation to your surroundings. Each direction, regardless of which you are traveling towards at the moment, is equally important to the destination you are charting.

The Communication Compass I've developed is also based on the four primary orientations, or directions, that we must take in our relationships to stay on course. Derived from those very simple lessons we have been taught by the geese, what follows are the four main characteristics that must exist in your relationship for it to thrive: Nurturing, Sharing, Encouraging and Working together. Structured together as a compass, NSEW, these

24

concepts are illustrated from a communication perspective, both verbal and non-verbal.

> **"Love does not dominate; it cultivates."**
> *Johann Wolfgang von Goethe*

Nurturing

"Something that nourishes or helps to grow, develop or cultivate."

Geese, as portrayed in the *"Lesson,"* demonstrate nurturing when two birds break formation to follow an injured bird down. They tend to the injured bird by protecting it and trying to nourish it back to health. They refuse to abandon it, until it either heals and returns to flight with the others, or dies. We can learn a lot, not only about teamwork in groups, as the *Lesson from the Geese* is often compared, but in close personal relationships as well. The absolute refusal, demonstrated so beautifully by the geese, not to take the easy way out and allow the injured bird to fend for his self, is really quite extraordinary. This instinctive behavior exhibited by the geese is a perfect example of expectancy. If there were an expectation that the injured bird would die, what would be the need for others to break out and follow? That expectancy, that if nurtured, the injured bird might survive appears to drive their actions.

As humans, most of us understand what nurturing is. When we feed and play with our pets, we are nurturing them. When we plant seeds, water, and cultivate them, we are nurturing them. As parents, when we teach our children and educate them, we are nurturing them. All of these things we do with an expectancy that in every case they will grow and thrive. In relationships, on the other hand, we typically have the expectation that each of us has had the proper amount of nurturing from others. We do not acknowledge the impact that this failure to nurture, not only each other, but our relationship as well, has on us. We are not meant to grow alone. Children need parents. Plants need soil and water. Pets need people. So why do we fail to recognize that we need to continue to nurture each other?

In both my Interpersonal Communication and my Introductory Speech classes, I typically begin by introducing my students to my Communication Compass. It has always been my belief that one cannot further any relationship if it is missing any of the four characteristics of Nurturing, Sharing, Encouraging and Working together. Clearly, then, the success of any relationship begins with your willingness to nurture it.

One of my favorite quotes is from Julius Ceasar "It is better to create than to learn! Creating is the essence of life." Many have contested this statement by saying learning is what is most important in life. Too many of us study and learn, though, without ever applying what we've learned to our own lives. This is what I've realized of myself these past couple of years. I studied, learned much, and then I began teaching to others what I had learned, never fully applying that knowledge to my own life. Only now, after experiencing the loss of divorce, have I made the correlation between creating and nurturing. When one gives birth to a child, creating a new life, nurturing becomes the continuum. Basically, we seek to continue to create by molding that child into the best possible person we can. But we don't seem to want to do this with our relationships.

How many times in our lives do we encounter words or concepts that have uniquely different connotations? It is said that terminology is often subjective. Just as "Aloha" can mean hello or goodbye depending on whether the person you are with is coming or going, "crabbing" I've discovered, is another word with two distinctly different meanings. Both of which, I've observed, have great significance when associated with close personal relationships.

Being an avid fisherman, I thought about how, when we go crabbing, we are able to draw the crabs in so easily. Then we toss them into a bucket and never need to put a lid on that bucket. Why? Because those crabs in the bucket, in a "King-of-the-Hill" competition, continuously pull each other down and not one ever escapes. In terms of relationships, the crab behavior is similar to having the ability to draw others to us based often on a false representation of our own self. These are expectations we want others to have of us. We toss people into our lives, so to speak, waiting to see if they are able to rise to the expectations we have of them. In essence, we have set a "bar" for them.

Generally, when you set a "bar" for someone, you have set an expectation for them that they may or not be able to meet. Or, as is often the case, a bar you may not want them to meet for fear that they will discover how easily they were drawn in with false expectations of you. When they fail to meet the expectations you have of them, you may become disappointed and disillusioned. Or if, much like the crabs pulling each other down, your intent all along was to keep them down. Setting any kind of expectation in a relationship demonstrates a complete lack of desire to nurture it. Without nurturing you fail to create any meaning in the relationship.

This reminds me of a video I watched of Viktor Frankl lecturing on the topic of "Man's Search for Meaning." Here Frankl discusses the term "crabbing" as it pertains to flying. He expresses to his audience how the same concept is applicable to how we should treat others. In the lecture, Frankl explains that in flying, you must be able to anticipate difficulty and deviation in wind patterns, how to do this you must put forth a bit of effort in calculating a higher trajectory to land where you want. He suggests a similar strategy in how we treat people, relating his theory to Goethe's most profound quote: "*Treat a man as he is and he will remain as he is. Treat a man as he can and should be, and he will become as he can and should be.*" In other words, don't set a bar for someone to try to reach; believe in them and make them believe they are already there! This is not only nurturing, this is creating. This is expectancy.

Positive feedback is, without question, a powerful motivator. Let's say, just as an exercise, you are attracted to someone based on their outer appearance, the "Halo Effect" we discussed earlier. You set an expectation, based on this appearance, that they possess more characteristics, such as a compatible intellect and interests. You, in turn, attract this person, and you begin a relationship. Conversations begin, and you discover that you are not as similar as you had thought in the beginning and you no longer feel a connection with this person. This generally happens when you live with expectations. If you engage this person, though, with an attitude of expectancy, what you are doing is not expecting anything. In *hoping* that they have compatible intellect and interests, you will open up and share more with them. In short, you nurture them by conveying the message that you see more in them!

If you apply this kind of "crabbing" to your relationships from the beginning the outcome can be more than you might ever expect, but it does require effort on your part to unlock the potential in others. Nurturing others creates meaning in your relationship with them. I have discovered, through teaching, that nothing unlocks more potential in a person than making them believe that they are more than *they* believe themselves to be.

Nonetheless, I'll be the first to admit I did not always nurture my wife. While I provided her financial support and security, I was not always supportive of her interests and ambitions. Did I not want to see her grow? Did I not want our relationship to grow? Of course I did. I just didn't understand at the time that nurturing is an essential action, or direction, that must be established in a relationship. I can say, with all honesty, that I never sought to fully understand her needs, or to fulfill them. I lived with expectations of what I wanted in a wife. She was with me through my college years, but I never asked her if there was something she desired to do. I never expressed any potential I believed she might have had. Did she want to attend college? Was there something she wanted from life other than what I perceived to be obvious, *me*?

In relationships, it seems, we usually wait for the other person to ask us to be supportive, to tell us what he or she wants or needs. Geese act instinctively. They provide support when there is an obvious need. We don't act instinctively because we look at ourselves as individuals, not as part of a team, even a team of two. We know what we want, and quite often assume that our partner is satisfied just being along for the ride.

The second primary aspect of nurturing, aside from believing in your partner, is to be supportive. One definition of supportive is *"to keep from weakening or failing."* We generally believe that we support each other in our relationships, but still they continue to weaken and fail despite our best intentions. Often we misunderstand what support means. It means to reinforce, to validate, and to sustain each other emotionally. Often, when relationships start to fail, we view support as sacrifice. *"I supported you through college and then..."* is really saying to your partner *"I gave up everything so you..."* This is, most emphatically, not nurturing communication. This only serves to elicit guilt from our partner and to provide one with a sense of justification for wanting to abandon a relationship, rather than to nurture it back to a healthy state.

It is important that you understand this; support is not sacrifice! It is the understanding that whatever each of you is doing independently, through school or career for example, benefits the relationship, your integrated identity, the "we." The emotions generally displayed as support are pride, satisfaction, and respect for the other's achievements. Emotional support provides far more value to a relationship than financial support. One of the deepest desires we all have as humans is the need for approval, which is another way of asking for support from those closest to us.

To be headed in the same direction, we must continue to nurture each other. We must identify the strengths and weaknesses in our partner as well as in our self. By believing in our partner and unlocking their potential we are helping him or her grow. Ultimately our relationship grows into a beautiful creation to share. A relationship can never be its strongest when either partner is at their weakest. I've come to understand from my own marriage that it was our weakness, our failure to nurture each other that caused the relationship to stop growing. Ultimately, this failure to nurture each other is what caused our relationship to end.

> **"Friendship marks a life even more deeply than love. Love risks degenerating into obsession, friendship is never anything but sharing."**
> *Elie Wiesel*

Sharing

"To participate in, use, enjoy, or experience jointly or in turns; to relate to another or others."

In their migration, geese instinctively take turns sharing responsibility. As the leading bird tires, and drops back from the head of the formation, another flies forward to fill the position. As humans we do not typically exhibit those same natural, voluntary instincts. We are not always quick to share the responsibility of keeping our relationships moving forward. We tend to sit back and expect that our partner will take the lead, instead of demonstrating, with expectancy, that if we act first we might achieve a more desirable outcome.

Sharing is undoubtedly one of the most complicated aspects of relationships. When we initially think of sharing, we think about giving something to someone in need: clothing, money, food, etc. Yet, in relationships, especially our most intimate ones, we associate sharing with only the verbal aspect: what we choose to disclose to our partner. Typically, we discuss our day, our work, or our interests with each other. Over time, we even begin to view those discussions as an obligation rather than as time together to anticipate and relish. Many of us, whether out of our desire for autonomy, or our desire to "prove" something to our partner, or maybe because we fear that our partner may actually take the lead in our endeavors, tend to keep secrets from each other. If we are to learn anything from what the geese teach us about sharing responsibility, we need to learn to accept that in any relationship -- friends, family or our most intimate ones -- we each have strengths and weaknesses and should seek to complement each other to achieve success in our relationship.

Failing, however, to understand the importance of disclosure in my nearly twenty year marriage, I realize the primary reason for this is because we are not always the best listeners. My wife, for example, graduated from high school with a full scholarship to college. Being that we were very young at the time, she gave up the scholarship, and any dream she may have had of attending college, because it would have taken her a good hour away from the town we both lived in. She chose, instead, to remain with me.

At that time, people were not accustomed to long distance daily commuting. Things like affordable cell phones, Skype, and Facebook were futuristic: the stuff of fiction. Even land line telephones were not a feasible alternative to remain close as this was considered long distance which, at that time, was very costly. "Long distance relationship" was a term not even coined until more recent years. Though she never really explained to me why she gave up her dream of college, I believe she gave it up to be with me. If she ever expressed a desire to me to have gone to college, I was selfish and was not listening. I would not have heard her.

> **"Wisdom is the reward you get for a lifetime of listening when you'd rather have been talking."**
> *Aristotle*

Later, as our family continued to grow, it became necessary for me to work multiple jobs to support us. During those years I never thought back to what she had given up for me, I just remember feeling frustrated, tired, and resentful that I was the only one working. Even if she had been able to find employment, with no degree or experience her income likely would not have even covered the outside costs of child care and transportation. Unlike the geese, I had to remain at the head of the formation alone. There was no one to step up and take some of the burden from me. At least that is how it how I perceived it to be.

Fast forward to this year as I sat wallowing in my own self-pity wondering why my relationship had collapsed. A woman I had once enlisted to try to help me build a website happened to come back into my life. We had only spent minimal time together, discussing the project, before conflicts in our work schedules caused us to lose touch for a couple of years. The project never materialized during this time, the same time that my marriage, a relationship of nearly 20 years, was ending. I shelved the website idea and went forward living day-to-day watching my life fall apart.

Liz, who I am now proud to call one of my best friends and my business manager, appeared for the second time in my life, at a time when I truly needed someone to help me turn my life around. Even though we had not seen each other for nearly two years she asked me right away if I had gone forward with my website. Despite the current state of my life, it shook me to the core to realize that someone I hadn't known for very long took an interest in something that I had long since pushed out of my thoughts. It was uplifting and I was eager to talk to her about all that was happening to me. Suddenly, the thoughts I had pushed aside for the website began to flow. One month after my divorce became final, and shortly after Liz and I reconnected, *Halo Again* began to develop from a dream into something tangible.

Even with this newfound resolve, this journey too, was to be a rocky road. Remember, I was still wallowing in self-pity. Liz, being a few years older, listened objectively to my ramblings and ravings, then verbally smacked me back into reality on numerous occasions. I'm not sure I've mentioned before (smile) that I am Italian, but as I expressed to her some of the issues my wife and I argued over and how heated the arguments could sometimes become, she would shake her head and ask me if I truly understood what love was. She pointed out a lot of self-serving ideas that I had concerning what I had expected from my relationship. I'll admit now that having reality presented to me the way she did, I began to realize that I could have done a lot more to preserve my relationship if I had ever honestly expressed my feelings, without spite, without anger, and truly listened to my wife instead of always reciprocating her anger.

Along the way, as *Halo Again* was unfolding, Liz began to struggle with the overall website concept due to the tremendous amount of material I was trying to incorporate, some as fast as I was learning it myself. What I wanted was a way to reach other people in relationships, to try to help them avoid the pitfalls I had encountered. Overwhelmed and frustrated, she called me one day and said that there was no way she could address this all in a website. That what I actually had was a story – a book. She had not been the first person to express this to me, but she was the one who expressed it the loudest.

Then something wonderful happened! She didn't walk away and throw her hands up saying the website wasn't possible. She didn't abandon me or the project we had begun. Instead, she jumped in and took the lead. I had been flying solo for so long that I didn't see that if someone truly cared, they would jump in and help me, even guide me to a better place in my life. I was very hesitant at first about sharing so much of myself to someone I hadn't known for very long. Over a period of about four weeks as I was preparing finals for my spring classes, she set in motion a series of events that ultimately led me to write this book. She took all of my emails, topics, and the presentations I had taught in my classes, and began organizing an outline for me. After classes ended for the semester, she presented all of it to me, organized into chapters, with about forty or so pages of content I had given to her over about two months and said, "See, now sit down and write the rest! You want people to learn from your mistakes, so tell them what they were."

She stayed with me throughout the entire project, learning on her own time the ins and outs of self-publishing, and using her strong organizational skills to keep me on track. The book quickly started to become a reality. She believed in me. She pushed me. She shared her time with me without any expectation of monetary compensation. Liz willingly shared her expertise to help me realize a dream. Over this last year I have grown to love her, as she has me, not in a physical way, but unconditionally as a friend and confidant. The beauty of our relationship is in what we share, what we bring out in each other. Freely sharing our time and talents with each other has made our lives better, both separately and together.

Liz now lives several states away, but because of what she shared with me, and brought out in me, I can see now what was missing from my marriage. If my wife and I had been willing to develop this kind of deep friendship, and loved each other unconditionally as Liz and I had been able to do -- without any expectations -- there would have been nothing we wouldn't have willingly shared. The strongest desire in our marriage should have been to contribute to, and witness each other's growth, and realize how that growth would have strengthened our marriage. Sadly, it seems, we can see the needs and dreams of those outside of our most intimate relationship more easily than we can those of our partner.

Looking back on what I have learned through this process, I wish that I would have sought to develop a stronger bond of friendship with my wife, instead of harboring only those expectations of what her role was to be in my life. I wish I would have chosen to help her achieve her dreams by sharing my time and my experiences. I wish I had lived my life with expectancy, to see what we could have become together if I had shared in her dreams and she had shared in mine. Love should never become an obligation, but instead remain a playground where together, like childhood friends, we joyously run, climb, and swing on each other's dreams.

"Truly great friends are hard to find, difficult to leave, and impossible to forget."
G. Randolf

Encouraging

"Giving confidence, promise or hope to."

The example of encouragement in the lesson learned from geese is how when flying in formation, the constant honking is to encourage those in front to keep up their speed. It is important to encourage -- to give hope or promise to -- not only the partner in your relationship, but to the relationship as well. As in the case of the geese flying in a formation, encouragement helps your relationship stay steady in its course. Encouragement also helps you seek new opportunities for growth. It is meaningful interaction. It is a loving expression of approval and support.

The opposite of encouragement, discouragement, is what a great deal of us demonstrate especially when someone we love deviates from our expectation of what the relationship is, or where our life together is going. Out of fear, we tend to discourage anything that empowers or promotes a sense of individuality in our partner. When we fear something, we tend to say what we want to say, and these comments are often negative. What we need to do is honestly express our feelings. When we feel emotionally injured by our partner, we lash out. We often initiate this pattern when we feel that something our partner is doing will make him or her look better to the outside world than we do. This is often perceived by us as our partner's need for change.

In the Introduction, I told the story of how my close friend saw the potential in me to become a teacher. For many years prior to that day, while working at Eastman Kodak, and throughout my college years, I used to share similar stories with my co-workers, always with the same enthusiasm and excitement. A few of my friends even began calling me "the Professor." I believe it was my love for sharing knowledge and interesting tales, the reinforcement I received from my co-workers, friends, and family along with that one "aha" moment when my friend declared that I should be a teacher, that provided me with the crucial encouragement I needed to become what I am today. Encouragement, then, is the essential component of interdependence.

Interdependence, the value on which I elaborate more in Chapter Eight, is commonly defined as a "reciprocal relationship between two or more independent entities." In the case of my wife and I, it is clear now that we did not have an interdependent relationship. When I sought her support, as I wanted to give up the work I had always done to begin teaching, she was not encouraging. She exhibited fear, as I described above, instead of support. I don't believe her reaction was intended to discourage me; I believe she was just reacting out of fear of the unknown. Would our income be the same? Could we make it if it was less? Whatever the reason was, I failed the relationship just as I felt she had. We both chose not to communicate, which was probably the beginning of what was to be the end.

This is not an uncommon occurrence in most people's lives. Men, for instance, often have issues with women earning a higher salary, or of having a higher ranking position or job title, than they do. Women often have issues with their husband if he wants to try something new, especially something that may result in lower pay or job status. Let's use, for example, a lawyer who wants to quit his job to start a landscape business. This change would likely result in lower pay. This, in turn, lowers the wife's perceived standard of living and represents, in her eyes, failure to the world. As a result, she may discourage instead of encourage. In this scenario, much as was my personal experience, by assuming her husband's dream is a step backward, the wife is failing to encourage him to reach his full potential. To not limit one another, to have shared his dream of planting evergreen gardens, who knows how successful they could become together? Therefore, be honest with yourself in these situations and ask "Am I discouraging my partner just as a reaction to fear of the unknown?"

We should never attempt to do anything other than encourage each other to pursue our ambitions, to achieve our goals, with expectancy for a stronger relationship and a better future. This enhances our shared identity. Encouragement, while not synonymous with, goes hand in hand with sharing. Encouragement and sharing make *you* a part of your partner's hopes and dreams. The alternative, discouragement, breeds an air of discontent, and opposition that may ultimately lead to the complete dissolution of your relationship, as I painfully learned.

Encouragement, though, may require compromise. *"Something intermediate between different things"* is the most appropriate definition of compromise applicable to relationship communication. We as humans are different, not only in our physical makeup, but also in our desires. Take, for example, my wife and I. I had my own dreams and ambitions. I expected her to nurture and encourage me to pursue my education and career. I expected her to take care of our home, our children, and all the associated domestic duties. I assumed that this was her dream too, because she never expressed anything other than that to me. I failed to see that she may have missed out on the opportunity to further her education, or to pursue a career, over the course of our twenty-year marriage. I never saw her as a true partner, one that needed equal encouragement from me, to pursue her dreams. Unfortunately, as I see now, I wasn't willing to compromise on my expectations.

Compromise does not necessarily have to be a negotiation. I am not referring to gaining some benefit for myself. I should have embarked on a voyage of discovery with her, to be willing to learn who she was, what she wanted to be, and allow her to become that *with* me. The compromise I needed to make was to look beyond myself and my needs, to allow her the same opportunities I had, college and career, or at the very least, open my eyes to the possibility that she had other needs.

W orking Together

*"A process where two or more people
collaborate to achieve a desired shared goal."*

The most significant lesson the geese teach us is that by flying together in formation, through this interdependence, they achieve a 71% greater flying range than if each bird flew on its own. Imagine how successful our relationships could be if we always worked interdependently with each other, instead of independent of each other. Imagine how much we would gain from this.

Nothing is more painful than suffering the collapse of a relationship because you or your partner failed to recognize in time that you did not try hard enough to make it work. A relationship must be a true partnership to succeed. You would never go into a business partnership with someone who did not share a common goal and the same work ethic needed to achieve success. Why, then, would you expect that a personal relationship would be any different?

Have you ever stepped back and looked at occasions in your life where working together with your partner was a clear sign of strength and harmony in your marriage or relationship? Or, as in my case, stop to reflect back on a particular life event that should have been a red flag indicator that you and your partner were heading toward an irreconcilable parting. In hindsight, this red flag indicator might have been counteracted using Communication Intelligence.

In 2007, I began the laborious task of building a brand new home for my family. I wanted to build this home for my family to show them how much I wanted to give to them; how much I loved them. From the first day construction began, however, until the day construction was completed, I felt like I was working alone in this project. My wife, while she occasionally stopped by and brought meals to me, never seemed very interested in working with me during the construction of our future home. I didn't let that bother me because, after all, I am Italian and this was man's work!

During this same period, I had a neighbor who was constructing a home on a nearby lot. Every day, it seemed, his family was there by his side. When the slab was poured I watched in amazement as his wife swept and vacuumed it clean every day when work concluded. As the walls were going up, I observed her with a shop-vac, cleaning the areas in the wall cavities, removing any dust and debris that had settled there. I observed their happy children giggling and waving paintbrushes as they helped their parents paint. Day by day, I watched them enviously as they shared that time together, looking happy to be working together on their project. I continued to believe, though, that what I was doing for my wife was all I needed to do to ensure our bond remained unbroken, and that she loved me.

I am not trying to initiate a "you poor thing" response here because only now as I write this do I realize that it was my neighbors who were truly communicating, verbally and non-verbally, through their actions towards each other. They truly had a relationship that was a partnership. They truly knew the value of working together. I had within me the same power to communicate with my wife, but I took no action. All along I lived with the *expectation* that what I was doing by building this home for my family was all I needed to do. I watched the other couple day-by-day, building their dream together. Every day I waited, *expecting* my wife to ultimately come around and want to do the same with me.

The idea never once occurred to me to scoop her up one day, and take her to have a picnic lunch on the foundation, quite literally, of what could have been our new life together -- to initiate a moment of excitement and invite her into the world that I had been working in alone. We had been married for nearly fifteen years at that point, and somewhere along the way, I failed to recognize the need to continually inspire or bring her into the project with me. I just *expected* her to want to.

I stated earlier that no one wants to think of a relationship as work. This is true. We only want fun in our relationships because let's face it - we already have to work hard in every other aspect of our lives. The truth is that wanting a good relationship is just like wanting a new car, or new shoes, or a special vacation. For those things, we are willing to work hard to ensure we are able to get what we want. Work can be fun and rewarding. We just need to be using the appropriate definition of work.

The most common association we make with work is *"a job, a task, employment."* At the end of the day, we are tired and don't want to work anymore. We just want the reward. The most romantic definition of work is *"an artistic creation,"* as in a work of art. The word "work" can become meaningful in, and to, our relationships if we look at it with expectancy, as creating something beautiful to be enjoyed and admired. Your relationship is truly an unfolding creation, where every day brings a new stroke to the canvas. The beauty in the creation comes from two hearts, and minds, working together, sharing the tasks needed to complete the work. Cleaning the brushes and protecting the canvas from damage. Yes, that's a fancy way of saying, guys help with the dishes or other household chores. In doing so, the two of you can share valuable time together: time to talk, time to play. Or, better yet, spend time in the kitchen preparing a meal together. We rarely ever even sit down to eat a meal together anymore. If you find yourselves home together, spend this time working together, preparing a meal, and then sharing the meal. You may find that you *can* make your cake and eat it too! More importantly, take advantage of these moments. Use them to connect. Put the wonder and excitement back into your lives before you are left wondering what happened, as I did, when I failed to include my wife in our life.

"You can discover more about a person in an hour of play than in a year of conversation."
Plato

Communication through actions, largely non-verbal, will speak volumes to your partner! It shows that you appreciate the work he or she puts into the relationship. In your own personal life and career, you do nothing without a purpose. While we work for the obvious, a paycheck, it is the appreciation we receive, the recognition for a job well done, or for an exceptional ability we have, that motivates us to learn and grow. In a relationship your partner needs the same from you. It does not necessarily need to come in verbal form, as I stated above. Just simply helping take dishes from the table to the kitchen, instead of wandering off to the living room to watch television alone, is sometimes all the appreciation that is needed.

You must learn to appreciate your partner's efforts frequently. As the song says, *"You don't know what you've got 'til it's gone."* It is easy to overlook the people closest to you, to not recognize them for what they do for you, to not place value on them. We tend, in relationships, to begin taking those closest to us for granted. People are constantly evolving. People constantly desire change to feel alive, but unless you want that change to be replacing you, you had better acknowledge that you are not the only one making this relationship what it is. Without assessing the partnership aspect we overlook, or fail to appreciate, those things we each contribute. We just expect them. You must express appreciation for everything your partner does for you and everything they mean to you. It takes so little effort and the reward is that you begin to see the interdependence gained from working together as partners.

For a compass to work properly, the needle must never get stuck. If it does, you may never be able to find out where you really are, or which direction you should be heading. Somewhere along my own personal journey, my wife and I lost sight of our compass, ultimately drifting in different directions. It is very clear to me now that in a relationship we can never reach our destination together if we are traveling alone. We must be united in our effort, sharing the responsibility of navigating through our journey together. It was the lessons the geese have taught me that posed the most interesting question: Who knew that the most loving, nurturing, encouraging and hardest working relationships on earth existed hundreds of feet in the sky? What a lofty goal for the rest of us.

CHAPTER TWO

The Inventory:

A.R.E. You Giving Your
Relationship What it Needs?

"There is nothing like rejection to make

you do an inventory of yourself."

James Lee Burke

- Chapter Two -

More long term relationships owe their success to expectancy than to expectation. Everyone, at one time or another, experiences a situation or circumstance that is out of their control. How we choose to embrace the issue determines whether we rise above the circumstance or we allow it to consume us. Issues that are addressed with expectation are often lost. This is because once we allow an expectation to dictate an outcome we look for no other possible resolutions. This applies not only to our relationships, but also to life in general. It is clear then, that we need to learn to overcome our issues with expectancy. To do this we must stop and take an inventory of our relationship. Before we do this, though, in order to determine if we have all the necessary requirements to see our journey together succeed I want to introduce you to the concept of *A.R.E. Language*.

The two most commonly demonstrated languages in interpersonal communication are "You" language and "I" language. "You" language is generally not considered appropriate in relationships because of its tendency to be accusatory, putting all the blame on your partner. "I" language is considered more appropriate in that it has you assuming responsibility for whatever is wrong. "I" language, however, can also backfire when used inappropriately. "I" statements can often cause your partner to become defensive if they feel that you are being condescending or patronizing.

An example of two similar statements using "You" language and "I" language that are both ineffectual might be: "You don't understand what I'm telling you." versus "I don't think I am making myself clear." Both statements can be perceived as derogatory, implying that the listener is incapable of comprehending what is being said. In a relationship, as in a conversation, there are always two sides, and if you are going to communicate effectively with each other, more than just the statements you make, your actions toward each other need to reflect that as well.

A.R.E. Language differs from both "You" and "I" language in that it is largely non-verbal. I've developed *A.R.E. Language* to help you understand that what you give to your relationship, and what your relationship needs, is directly based on how you communicate both verbally and non-verbally with your partner. **A**ction, **R**eaction and **E**xpectancy make up the three components of *A.R.E. Language*.

It wasn't until my marriage ended that I became acutely aware that the direction we *A.R.E.* heading is directly related to the language we *A.R.E.* using. Scholars, and textbooks, tell us that more than half of our communication is non-verbal. It is not surprising, then, that statistics show a significant amount of negative communication is presented in a relationship without either partner ever uttering a single word.

If your relationship is off-course, and you are drifting in a direction that is going nowhere, now is the time to stop and evaluate your position. To determine a new direction, gather your supplies, and chart your new course together by taking an inventory. If you do not take an inventory and you are in short supply of any necessary provisions, in life, as in sailing, the journey may end before you reach your destination just as mine did. Using *A.R.E. Language* will allow you to identify your expectations in order to address them with expectancy. To replace these expectations you need to be able to alternately identify any issue or situation as an opportunity instead of a problem.

"You don't develop courage by being
happy in your relationships every day.
You develop it by surviving difficult times
and challenging adversity."
Epicurus

The Halo Effect, as described in Chapter One is partially, if not mostly, responsible for the actions and reactions we exhibit based on the expectations we have in our relationships. Those misguided expectations we form in the beginning of most relationships that leave us feeling unhappy when our partner fails to meet up to them. In turn, when we are unhappy we begin to display negativity in both our actions and our reactions. The Halo Effect limits us, in most of our relationships, to see only what we believe we see them to be. The Halo Effect does not allow us to recognize what the relationship truly is, or has the potential of becoming. Instead we should learn to recognize the potential of others and what they can bring to our relationships, even when that potential is not immediately apparent. This expectancy keeps us motivated to keep the relationship growing.

With my wife, I realize now I did nothing to help her change or grow. I wanted her to remain as I saw her in the beginning. I wanted her to, I realize now, fulfill those expectations I had set based on my initial perceptions of her. There was no way our relationship could succeed. It was, as she pointed out to me near the end, destined to fail. This is how I've come to discover that expectancy, not expectation, is the basis on which we should form our relationships and establish effective communication within those relationships.

**"Who is richer? The man who is seen,
but cannot see? Or the man who is
not being seen, but can see?"**
Babe Ruth

Expectancy allows us to place value on what we hope our relationship will become as we grow together as a couple. There are many situations in which we allow negative expectations to prevail -- job loss, relationship breakup, discrimination, failed business ventures, etc. In the following pages I will share examples that I learned on my own and that I've learned from others of how to win with expectancy instead of losing to expectation.

$\underline{A}$ction

*"The fact or process of doing something,
typically to achieve an aim".*

The purpose of any action is to get a reaction. Little that we do, or say, in our relationships happens by accident. It is our nature as human beings to act with purpose. The trick is to identify what that purpose is. Purposes drive our actions, something we all learn as children when we first try to get our parents to react to us. Children, even as infants, are instinctively better able to gauge what actions are required to get the responses they desire than we are as adults. If children are hungry or need changing, they scream. If children do not want something we have given them, they scream and throw it to the floor. If children want something we haven't given them, they scream while reaching out to that something with their arms open. If they don't want to do something we tell them to, they scream, "No!"

There is no purpose, in any relationship, that should involve controlling, berating, or repressing each other, yet we see people doing it all the time. While they may, or may not, be aware of it, these people believe that the purpose of entering into a relationship is to make their partner become what they expect him or her to be. In these relationships, the more aggressive, dominant partner has a tendency to intimidate the passive partner, usually in front of family and friends, to demonstrate this control. Sometimes the dominant partner will deny or ridicule the passive partner for wanting to try something new, especially if it isn't on the dominant partner's relationship agenda. If you want a relationship to succeed, and the

57

actions to become positive, it is imperative that you neither allow yourself to fall victim to this type of behavior, nor present it to your partner or others either verbally or non-verbally.

I can cite numerous times in my own relationship where my negative actions signaled disapproval or disappointment to my wife when I did not get what I wanted. After all, I believed I was the boss. The essential purposes of entering into a relationship should be to share a life together, to love unconditionally, to be loved unconditionally, and to be respected. If our relationships are to succeed, we need to stop looking just for someone to make *us* happy, we must in turn, be willing to make our partners happy and to respect them. And remember, the only true boss is Bruce Springsteen!

"We must learn to live together as brothers, or perish together as fools."
Martin Luther King, Jr.

It is true that actions speak louder than words, and are spoken much more frequently. In non-verbal communication, our actions are the most critical component of communication in the relationship. Often, in relationships, we get complacent. We assume that our partner is content just knowing we are there. As time passes from the initial stage of the relationship, when everything is new and full of wonder, we stop doing the little things that keep the sparks alive. Indifference begins to set in. Men no longer walk around the car to open the door for their wife. Women no longer concern themselves with asking *"How was your day?"* And almost no one takes the time anymore to hug or hold hands. A hug is one of the most comforting feelings you can imagine. That sweet, yet subtle, form of intimacy creates a sense of belonging simply by its definition *"To hold closely to."* Today, a lot of us often relegate all forms of physical intimacy, even hugs, to the bedroom. Beyond that, we may also set time limits to our physical intimacy, turning what was once passion to an obligatory action...and we *wonder* when, and why, the fairy tale ended? We don't touch each other enough anymore, therefore, we don't reach each other enough anymore.

I've discovered, through *Halo Again*, the imperative to recognize that every action we take has a direct impact on the overall health of our relationship. I have also discovered that based on the positivism or negativism of that action, the reaction can be predicted. We need to erase the term *"pick your battles"* from our collective consciousness, and realize that we don't need to have battles. Most battles start in relationships when someone wants something and somehow expects the other to know this automatically. If you want a hug, give a hug. If you want a conversation, start a conversation. It's very simple, just stop waiting each other out to see who goes first!

"If you wish to be loved, love."
Lucius Annaeous Seneca

So how do we begin to take <u>A</u>ction? How do we change "We have a problem" to "We have an opportunity" in our relationship?

Expectation – *We have a problem!*

Normal reactions, anger, anxiety, and ambivalence to situations we cannot control, are typically displayed when an expectation is present. Anger presents as an expectation that something has been "done" to you, even when you may have had some hand in causing the situation. Anxiety presents as an expectation that nothing can be done to resolve the issue, indicating a refusal to accept what has happened and move on. And ambivalence, or "mixed feelings," presents as an expectation that you have reached an end and you become indifferent to the situation at hand.

Let's talk about a typical relationship breakup. We can certainly say that we all naturally tend to experience anger first. The expectation that there is nothing we can do, that the fault lies with our partner, is often where our emotions take us in the beginning, followed immediately by anxiety. We experience anxiety over not only the loss, based on an expectation of failure that we believe has occurred and is irrevocable, but also over a fear of moving on. Finally, ambivalence sets in, and we experience the love/hate syndrome, and now a new expectation forms in you that all relationships will end in the same fashion.

Expectancy – *We have an opportunity!*

While little can be done to avoid the initial reactions we all experience, as they live within us and are defined as "human nature," we can learn to overcome the negativity of expectations. Expectancy is something we can teach ourselves and adapt to as each new situation arises in our lives. While this may sound like nonsense to some, it is relatively easy to achieve if you truly want to live a more fulfilling life. How do you do this? You learn to view your problems as opportunities.

In the case of a relationship breakup, you might start by asking what caused the break, and what it is that is making you so angry. Without question, some relationships are not able to be repaired. Often two people move in different directions, or outside influences, not always good ones, cause rifts in relationships.

Back to the *Halo Effect*, you may only enter a relationship based on appearances and immediate excitement, but when the newness wears off, you realize that there never was a strong foundation to build from. What is worse is that too often, either you or your partner may never have intended to build it in the first place. If you value your relationship, but consider yourself the wounded party in the breakup, you will typically manifest the expectations listed before. Instead of remaining angry and setting the expectation that all relationships might end this way, ask some simple questions:

- Do I want to try to work on repairing the relationship?
- If not, can I see how my actions might have contributed to the breakup?
- (Expectancy) What have I learned from this situation (problem) and can I take what was good in the relationship and start fresh (opportunity)? If not, how can I alter my future actions to make my next experience (opportunity) better?

If you truly want to repair your relationship, replace the anger you feel with hope. Think about what you believe caused the breakup. Identify how you, and the expectations you had, might have contributed to the breakup, and what actions on your part are necessary to breathe new life into the relationship. Remember, it is generally not one person's fault a relationship ends because there are always two people involved. When we are hurting, our natural tendency is to believe that we are the injured party. It is equally important to remember that your partner most likely feels the same way you do.

Having expectancy instead of expectation, can allow your actions to remain positive despite any negative reaction you may get from your partner. It is true that you cannot force others to feel the same way, but remember, if anything is to change for the better you have to abandon the expectations that limit you. If reconciliation is not possible, you simply need to remember that your next relationship does not have to meet the same fate. Not if you are willing to enter it, and maintain it, with hope and a positive spirit.

Reaction

"A person's ability to respond physically and mentally to external stimuli".

In relationships, we tend to display only negative reactions to our partner's actions when those actions are, or are perceived by as, negative. It is very hard, in relationships, to take a negative action and respond in kind with a positive reaction, but we should always try. Our human tendency, unfortunately, is to reciprocate equally. We attract a positive reaction to a positive action, and in the spirit of *"an eye for an eye"* we respond with a negative reaction to a negative action. We choose to fight fire with fire, instead of with water.

I present to my class, when I teach Interpersonal Communication, the powerful message conveyed in the movie *Fireproof.* Everyone in a relationship should watch this movie once. The premise of this movie is that in a failing relationship, the partner who sees the relationship as a failure, who wants out the most, is the one who needs to learn to react to every negative with a positive. In this movie, as was the case in my relationship, the man saw his wife's withdrawal from him as a personal affront. Initially, he did not desire to seek a solution to the problem, he simply wanted out of the relationship. Challenged by his father to test his capacity for tolerance, he was, in the end, able to reverse his situation through a method called the *"Love Dare."* It is basically the lesson I learned too late, but the lesson that effectively relays the message I am trying to send through this book -- that through the reactions you return, despite the actions directed at you, you may surprise your partner and the course of your relationship can be changed.

As I do with my classes, I encourage you to watch this movie, *Fireproof (2008, Kirk Cameron and Erin Bethea.)* I could never sum up the impact of actions and reactions more eloquently than this movie does. It demonstrates to us that even if things seem hopeless, if love ever truly existed in your relationship it is possible for one partner's actions to alter the reactions of the other partner. Ultimately, by doing so, it can change the entire direction of the relationship.

"A life of reaction is a life of slavery, intellectually and spiritually. One must fight for a life of action, not reaction."
Rita Mae Brown

So how do we overcome our tendency to **R**eact negatively in a stressful situation? How do we change "What will we do?" to "We can handle anything!" in our relationship?

Expectation – *What will we do?*

While anger, anxiety, and ambivalence are the common, initial reactions we have when we encounter situations we cannot control, they are often followed by ridicule, resentment, and risk. Looking back now to the aforementioned breakup, what is our most common reaction when we break up with someone? We make jokes about the other person, more often than not extremely hurtful jokes, believing that somehow this makes us the winner. Ridicule, if continued, quickly becomes an action instead of a reaction - an action we begin to believe validates our expectation that we have somehow won something, not lost something.

We begin to look to those in our circle of friends to support us, and not our partner. Even worse, we often look to those who have been close to both partners in the relationship for unconditional support. When we feel a lack of support from anyone in our circle, the pattern could repeat itself. For now we feel resentment towards not only our partner in this separation, but to those who would align with him or her. The final counterintuitive reaction is that we make a conscious choice to risk alienating not only our former partner, but also others who now see us as vindictive, cruel, and less likely to form a life-long partnership. Ironically, a negative expectation they now have of you!

Expectancy – *We can handle anything!*

Certainly, breaking up with someone is never easy, but what our expectations have set us up for is: the inability to consider reconciliation, the need to blame someone else for the breakup, and a bleak future in relationship building. This will become a truth, especially if we develop a pattern, one clearly noticeable to others, that our ultimate expectation is that relationships will generally end badly.

So, can we overcome this? Absolutely! By setting the expectancy that no matter what the outcome of the relationship, we have learned something, and gained value from what we have shared together. To have this expectancy from the start of a relationship helps to ensure that good can come from shared experiences, even in cases of loss. Expectancy is, in fact, key to avoiding a break up in the first place and can never be achieved unless you are willing to communicate and share feelings openly and honestly throughout the relationship.

Remember, expectations are simply assumptions we don't feel the need to share. Unlike expectancy -- a state in which we are hopeful of the end result -- with expectations, we are certain of the end result. Expectancy gives us that *"we can handle anything"* attitude because we always believe there is hope. We are willing to put forth that extra effort to work at our relationships and accept that some good comes from every situation. Expectancy shows us that every cloud does have a silver lining if you allow yourself to see it.

Expectancy

"Hoping that something, especially something pleasant, will happen".

Unlike *expectation, "something anticipated, whether feared or longed for,"* expectancy creates less conflict in our relationships. It is clear that our emotions, often difficult to control, need to be guided by intelligence, as do our expectations. We all have a tendency to set expectations - let's call them predictions – for, and of, our partner's behavior. The first type of expectation, those we set for someone else's behavior, is a controlling action. This is a negative action, one designed to constrain the other person. An example of this would be the expectation that certain responsibilities in a relationship fall to one partner exclusively, and that the other has the right to criticize, or berate, when that expectation is not met.

The second type of expectation, that which we expect of someone else, is generally based on assumptions. In the example above, the non-compliant partner might assume (expect) that the reaction from the dominant partner will be critical, and/or negative, no matter what they do. Always feeling forced to comply, the non-compliant partner will, sooner or later, grow tired of the constraints and abandon the relationship. This is the exact opposite of what working together in a relationship is all about.

There is a concept in the business world known as the Expectancy Theory, developed in 1964 by Victor H. Vroom of the Yale School of Management. It proposes that individuals will behave a certain way based on the desirability of the outcome of their actions. In business, this theory emphasizes "the needs for organizations to relate rewards directly to performance and to ensure that the rewards provided are those rewards deserved, and wanted, by the recipients." It is plausible, then, that we need to apply expectancy similarly to our relationships. That is, our actions (performance) should serve to elicit positive reactions (rewards).

There is no question that every action in our relationship is typically based on what we expect the reaction to be. Men, traditionally, seem to have more expectations of gender role responsibilities, so I'll continue to use my domestic analogies (as cliché as they are), to explain my reason for replacing expectations with expectancy in relationships.

Come on guys, if you are reading this, we all know we understand expectancy when it suits us. We are hopeful of a desirable outcome when we bring her flowers, aren't we? The rest of the time, going back to what society has programmed into us, we tend to set expectations which are in essence demands. This results in unhappiness for both partners when those demands are not met.

Expectations are generated as the result of things we either perceived (Halo Effect), or do not see in, but wish to change in our partner, to make them conform to some idealistic reality we want for our relationship. You cannot force another individual to change, but as we learned from Viktor Frankl, by believing in their potential we are opening them, as well as ourselves, up to new possibilities. *Halo Again*, the compass that guides us, serves to contradict the Halo Effect by causing us to look deeper not only into our partner, but also into our relationship as a whole. It is conceivable that by nurturing, sharing, encouraging, and working together, we are not only hoping for a positive outcome, but are creating a life-long relationship.

"I do my thing, and you do your thing. I am not in this world to live up to your expectations, and you are not in this world to live up to mine. You are you and I am I, and if by chance we find each other, it's beautiful."
Frederick E. Perls

Here is where we must ultimately learn to overcome expectation with expectancy, and replace "Will we struggle with this?" with "We are on another adventure!" in our relationship.

Expectation – *Will we struggle with this?*

Often a lack of communication in our relationship, especially in situations that couples often break up over, like financial troubles, causes us to feel that there is no hope or future with our partner. This expectation, or lack of hope, leaves us with feelings of emptiness, exposure, and exasperation.

When most of us feel a struggle coming on we want to avoid it at all costs. Often that cost is ultimately the end our relationship. We often begin to rationalize that finding someone new and starting over (expectation/ assumption) will wash away the emptiness.   That somehow this new person will allow us to regain our sense of invulnerability.   Once we feel exposed in a relationship, we assume we have lost some control and feel that the relationship could never be the same again. These expectations can lead us to a feeling of exasperation that we believe we can never overcome. Even worse, we allow this perceived need to move on to another relationship drive our actions.

Expectancy – *We are on another adventure!*

I know that turning struggles into adventures may seem impossible to some of you, but look back at the long history of fairy tales and fables written around struggles that ultimately led to wonderful happiness. You read them because they gave you hope, and because you wished that your life could turn out so beautifully. I know it sounds cliché to say to simply replace your expectations with expectancy, but isn't the extra effort worth it if the end result is happiness?

Very simply, take each situation and look back to the beginning of your relationship when you felt that nothing could stop the two of you. Unless you were born with a silver spoon, generally the beginning of a relationship is where you may encounter financial struggles, which you weather together as you begin to build your life. During that time, working together, you see your life as one big adventure. How, together, you will acquire the things you want in life: house, furnishings, family, and extravagances such as jewelry, exotic cars or even travel. If the situation that is tearing you apart now is financial, for example the result of a job loss, it is the tendency to view the situation as desperate and you may start to blame each other.

Take a breath, step back, close your eyes and go back to an earlier time when you didn't have the things or lifestyle you may have become accustomed to. Remember the excitement you shared together with every promotion or raise, with every new purchase, or with every trip you took together? If you could weather the storm then, try to look at the present situation with hope.

Most of us tend to view setbacks as failures or loss. By looking, together, at this setback as a new adventure you might even regain some of the passion you had in the beginning of your relationship, not only for each other, but the passion you had watching your life grow together. Embrace what is happening and together begin to create new dreams for your new future. Don't react...act!

The Inventory

So now we understand how our actions and reactions impact the expectancy we have for our relationships. *Halo Again* can show you how, by shifting into this mindset of expectancy, you can help each other deliver, and receive, more positive reactions whether the actions put forth are presented as a positive or a negative.

Now is the time to take an inventory of your relationship. So how do you do that? Using the template I've given you at the end of this chapter, you will answer questions on how you feel about your relationship and its present state. In this template, you will be asked to give your relationship a name. While I have provided some examples on the inventory worksheet, I encourage you to be creative here. For example, I refer to my former marriage as "Anchors Away."

Then, using drawings or verbal imagery, create a sketch of how you feel about your relationship. I based mine on a painting that I made in an art class some time ago (next page). I remember many times feeling anchored in the water, still and not moving...with others all around me, but not with me. All the while I wanted to lift the anchor I believed held me down and set sail alone...to abandon the relationship, as I felt my wife had already done.

Whether you look at your relationship with humor, or are saddened or even angered by its current state as I was, be honest with yourself. Regardless of how negative the label you give your relationship is now, the purpose of the inventory is to find out what is missing, and acquire the necessary provisions to continue the journey.

"**Anger: an acid that can do more harm
to the vessel in which it is stored than to
anything on which it is poured.**"

Lucius Annaeous Seneca

I teach Interpersonal Communication and this inventory is a tool I developed for my class to use to evaluate their relationships, especially if they have a relationship that they feel they need to improve. I encourage you to begin to evaluate your own relationship here. As you progress through this book, you will see that some of the labels you assign, or attribute as failures of your partner may, in fact, be your own failures.

> **"It is the peculiar quality of a fool to perceive
> the faults of others and to forget his own."**
>
> *Cicero*

Very often it is our tendency, until outside influences persuade us, to see life from our own perspective. If you allow this book to guide you, before you take drastic action as I did, and suffer a loss as I did, you may find that only a little patching is required for your vessel (relationship) to reach the treasure (love and happiness) that you seek.

After you complete the inventory assessment, you should return to it periodically. Using this inventory and the guide in the next chapter, as well as the insights I will provide in the remaining chapters, I hope to help you to see that what you perceived as a failure can be attributed to miscommunication; to see that it really is possible to change the course of your relationship if you are willing to put forth the effort.

COMMUNICATION COMPASS INVENTORY

➤ Select a relationship you would like to improve:

[ ] SPOUSE/PARTNER   [ ] DATING
[ ] CLOSE FRIEND   [ ] OTHER: _____

➤ Give your relationship a name that best describes how you feel about it (for example 'bosom buddies", "frenemies", "everlasting love", "anchors away", etc.):

_____

➤ Select the characterization that best describes the present state of this relationship or make up your own:

[ ] HAPPY/FULFILLING   [ ] COMPLACENT/STABLE
[ ] NEEDS WORK   [ ] DYSFUNCTIONAL
[ ] ENDING   [ ] OTHER: _____

➤ Use images to sketch or words to create labels that best describe your relationship:

➤ What areas do you feel need the most improvement? And state how you might act on them in the future (select all that apply):

NURTURING [ ] _____

_____

SHARING [ ] _____

_____

ENCOURAGING [ ] _____

_____

WORKING TOGETHER [ ] _____

_____

77

CHAPTER

THREE

How to Effectively

G.U.I.D.E. Your

Relationship

"Love...Force it and it disappears. You cannot will love nor even control it. You can only guide its expression. It comes or it goes according to those qualities in life that invite it or deny its presence."

David Seabury

- Chapter Three -

Every ship's captain needs a compass to **G.U.I.D.E.** him in order to navigate to any given destination. Relationships are mostly based on arriving at a shared emotional destination. The compass, introduced in Chapter One, serves to set or change the direction of your relationship based on the needs you both have. In this chapter, you will use the compass to **G.U.I.D.E.** you further on your journey, to help you to determine what stage you are at in your relationship. This chapter relates the importance of setting and achieving goals together and identifies where the compass needle should be pointing to help you navigate to, and through, each stage of your relationship.

In the years I have taught Interpersonal Communication, I have presented to my classes the traditional relationship stages, illustrated in the textbook as a step pyramid. On one side, the steps going up indicate the stages of the growing relationship. When you reach the top, you have passed through each of the stages that created the relationship and have reached the plateau, or maintenance level. Then, all that is left (no pun intended) is the *down side*, where the relationship begins to come apart if not properly managed. This model, while traditionally accepted, is based on expectation and not expectancy. There is never a down side with expectancy, only hope.

Based on this observation, I have identified five primary stages of relationships as follows: **G**rowth, **U**nderstanding, **I**dentity, **D**iversity, and **E**xperience. Knowing what each of these stages represents in your relationship, and acknowledging that combined they represent a circle and not a straight line or pyramid as others describe them, is not only helpful for strengthening existing relationships, but also for dealing with change.

"He who loves practice without theory is like the sailor who boards ship without a rudder and compass and never knows where he may cast."
Leonardo da Vinci

As we are all aware, change is inevitable in relationships because as individuals *we* are ever-changing. What we need, and what we want, changes over time but that change does not have to lead to disillusionment and discontent in our relationships. Disillusionment is typically the result of unmet expectations, so it is important that we learn to adapt to each and every change throughout our journey with expectancy - *with hope*!

Throughout each stage you will use the compass to **G.U.I.D.E.** you on a different heading; a different stop along your journey. If you carry the positive elements of each stage of your developing relationship into each subsequent stage, you will ultimately find you come full circle. Each change you experience can bring you back to a new Growth Stage; a new beginning, with new expectancy for the continually unfolding creation that is your relationship. I hope to help you see exactly how, by embracing change with expectancy, you can bring value and many more years to your relationship!

It is very important to remember that not every relationship is destined to be *"the one."* You know that soul-mate that we all believe exists and will appear, as if by magic, in our life. Some of our intimate relationships are just passing encounters and may fizzle out early. Some develop into strong, even life-long friendships. All, however, require a level of understanding, as well as interest and dedication, to see whether or not they will evolve.

Learn to look beyond the expectations you may have set for the relationship, and ask yourself what it is that you *hope* for. Before you can determine what stage that your relationship is presently in, it is important to first be certain that you have a healthy and meaningful connection, and that the feelings you are experiencing are mutual. If you have been trying to force a relationship to be what you want it to be, you are not truly considering the other person's needs and desires, you are only looking at your own needs and desires.

Any relationship, if based primarily on expectations, will generally fail within the Growth Stage, or if not, will likely fail by the time you reach the Diversity Stage. It is important to understand that it is possible for two people to love each other differently. Expectancy allows you to be honest about what your relationship is, and not look at the relationship for what it is not. If it is truly love then you both will feel the same way, but even if one of you feels stronger feelings initially, relationships can change along the way. Expectancy allows the relationship room to grow, and it may even surprise you just how much more it can!

"Because someone doesn't love you the way you want them to doesn't mean they don't love you with all they have."

Unknown

Instead of referring to the many different relational stages proposed by others, I am going to offer some insight into what I have discovered along my journey. To explain what you can do through the five stages I have identified, to make every day of your life together one to cherish as much as the first. To help you realize throughout each phase that you need to refer to the compass often in order to determine what direction you might need to take if at any time you feel that your relationship is drifting off course.

Growth

Phase 1: You focus and devote most of your time and energy on each other.

Growth is the initial stage of your relationship, often identified by others as the *"Romance Stage,"* the *"Courtship & Infatuation Stage,"* the *"Honeymoon,"* among others. Here is where your journey together begins. This is when you meet that someone new and your primary objective is to win that person over. In order to do that, you embark on a rigorous campaign to sell yourself. There is seemingly no limit to what you will do for this person. Generally, the other person has the same objective and is riding on the same tidal wave of thrill and passion.

Here is where you both pull out all the stops. Men will lavish women with flowers and jewelry, while women will give in to all of their man's desires by dressing to excite him, and by flaunting him to their friends - an intense form of flattery. The world circling about you both seems surreal. You are flooded with endorphins that create an intoxicating sensation that you both refuse to believe could ever end. Due to our cultural acceptance of premarital sex and instant gratification, a lot of relationships, even marriages, are conceived at this point before reality sets in and life takes over. Whether knowingly, or unknowingly, our initial actions are based on expectations and not expectancy. We are presenting our self to our partner as what we believe the other expects us to be. In doing so, we also set expectations for our self of our partner based on what he or she is presenting to us at that moment.

Remember, in the long run you can never achieve lasting happiness through fantasy or infatuation. In a healthy relationship based on expectancy it is the effort you each put into the other person, exploring each other, helping each other discover who each of you is. Discovering who you will become and where you are going together. In order to truly begin your journey, and set your relationship on the right course, you will need to use the compass to navigate successfully through each phase.

The Growth Phase, on the communication compass, begins with *Sharing*. Sharing serves to establish the foundation on which the relationship is to be built. Honesty in what you share with each other will ensure that the foundation of your relationship does not suffer major cracks over time. Representing our self as anything other than who we truly are will ultimately lead to mistrust.

One stereotypically humorous scenario of pretenses leading to failure of a relationship (often played out in television sitcoms) would be that of a relatively simple-looking insurance salesman representing his self to be successful and wealthy to a very attractive woman. The woman, in turn, represents herself to be a successful socialite when she is actually a school teacher who prefers more to read about social events than be thrust into them. Get where I'm going with this? Neither of them is basing their role in this relationship on what the other truly is, and has to offer; only what they pretend to have and offer – which ironically is what they each assume to be what the other person wants. They soon tire of maintaining the pretenses and realize that the relationship is ultimately not what either one wanted in the first place. As is often the ending in these sitcom episodes, they live happily ever after once they share the truth of who they are and discover they are both basically simple people with similar dreams.

Unfortunately, real life does not work this way for most of us. The expectations we have do not allow us to look beyond the pretenses. We are disappointed when the expectations we have are not met. This happens because we all have some expectation of finding the halo of perfection over those we would seek to have an intimate relationship with.   Initially, we are often seeking excitement and fail to see this person as a friend. A friend being a person we would value highly because of how they enrich our lives.

Why is this important? It is important because in the beginning of any relationship our primary objective should be to become friends first.   Friends are those people we trust enough to allow them to see us for who we really are. The truest marker of whether a relationship can last is whether or not we trust the other person enough to allow him or her to get this close us. If you are not honest from the onset of a relationship, you may find it difficult to regain the trust of your partner later.

I realized, much too late, that I had never truly been friends with my wife. If I had I would have never have held back anything from her. Like most people, I was all too willing to share my frustrations, as well as my desires, with others…with my so-called best friends. Women do this as well with their girlfriends. We are willing to share intimate details of our relationship, and where it is heading, with anyone other than our partner. Your partner should be the one person you *want* to share everything with about your relationship and where it is going. No matter how long you have been in, or remain in your relationship, it is important to always remember that in the beginning you should become friends first. Very often what we lose along the way, in our relationships, is the ability to take criticism from our partner like we would from our friends.

"A friend is one that knows you as you are, understands where you have been, accepts what you have become, and still, gently allows you to grow."
William Shakespeare

Open your mind with expectancy if you are in, or beginning a relationship. Be true to who you are and recognize that someone can only truly love you for what you are, not for what you pretend to be. I believe my own relationship failed partly because of the facade I may have displayed in the beginning, but failed to live up to in her eyes, and partly because of the expectations I set for my wife, based on my initial impression that I too believed she failed to live up to. While I waited too long, in hindsight I have learned that it is never too late to try to begin an existing relationship again. If I had lived with expectancy, instead of expectations in my marriage, that hope for a better future, for reconciliation, might have saved my marriage.

"Real love stories never have endings."
Richard Bach

If you are experiencing discontent in a relationship that may have been formed based on expectations, invite your partner to go on another "first date." Share your hopes for the relationship with him or her. Talk about what originally attracted you to them. Talk about what you may have misrepresented about yourself based on what you believed they expected of you. As I've stated before, however, don't just talk. It is very important that you listen as well. If you are willing to begin anew, you must be willing to stop trying to travel backward in time looking for a way to blame. Let go of any expectations you may have set based on *"what you are used to."* A new future brings new hope to a relationship, while expectations will ultimately lead to discontent.

$\underline{U}$nderstanding

Phase 2: You learn as much as possible about each other over the next few months or years.

Here is where others might start to disagree on what the 2nd stage of the relationship is. Some refer to this as the *"Power-Struggle"* stage. This is the stage where you may be becoming a little disillusioned with certain facets of the relationship, especially if you feel the expectations you entered the relationship with are not being met. You have taken off the rose-colored glasses. If you haven't already married by this point, this is where a lot of casual or short-term relationships end. If you have taken the leap to marriage, then this is truly the time to discover what makes each of you tick. No longer, it seems, are you willing to conform to what you initially believed the other wanted from you. Since, however, you have embarked on this journey together, it is time to set aside expectations and replace them with a new level of expectancy. Begin to actively learn about, and understand your partner, using this knowledge to envision a hopeful new future together. The Understanding Phase, on the compass, moves the relationship from Sharing to Encouraging.

Just as in the Growth Phase, you must continue to share with each other who you truly are, and what your dreams and ambitions are. If the relationship is not just a passing encounter and progresses from the Growth Phase, you need to be sure that you not only know your partner, but yourself as well. Often, we are so smitten with one another at the onset of a relationship that we don't recognize the importance of disclosure. I don't mean to sound ominous, what I'm saying is that we shouldn't be so quick to hold back disclosing any of our dreams or desires out of a fear of rejection or ridicule. Eventually these dreams will come out, and if they are something you have kept to yourself for a long time, your partner will see it as, and later fear it as, "change."

Understanding also means that you may each develop new interests along the way. As I stated earlier, this phase of the relationship is part of a larger circle so you may return here many times. This stage should never be considered a *"power-struggle."* A healthy relationship should be based on mutual emotional sharing, encouragement, and expectancy in order to create a lasting, supportive union.

"The key to any change is letting go of fear."
Rosanne Cash

If you share early, and often with each other instead of fearing "change," you may be surprised to find that both of you are more than willing to encourage your partner to pursue their ambitions. For example, someone who dreams of being an actor, but works as an accountant, might not want to share that desire with a new or current partner, or even a close friend, fearing ridicule. The difference in the perception of their dream often depends on the timing of the sharing. You should never be made to feel ashamed of any dreams or aspirations, or be forced to limit your unique potential.

If you share your dreams when you enter a new relationship, such as those of acting, they might be met with, "Wow, how exciting, I have a friend in the local theater!" or "Have you ever been in or considered auditioning for a local play?" Anyone who would ridicule, discourage, or make you feel the need to keep your dreams hidden will most likely not end up being your life partner, let alone a true friend. On the other hand, if you choose to hide your desires and reveal them later, say ten years into the relationship, this revelation will most likely be met with suspicion or doubt, or be perceived as a "mid-life crisis." Don't let your assumptions of what the other might be thinking determine what you choose to share and what you choose to hold back from each other. Expectancy, most certainly, goes hand in hand with honesty and openness.

Making assumptions about what the other person wants in a relationship is something we all commonly do, but it is a pitfall we must learn to overcome. You must be able to honestly tell each other what you want from the relationship and from each other. Assumptions are typically based on the expectations you may have set for one another, so be willing to discuss the role these expectations have played in the relationship and how to avoid making assumptions in the future by keeping the lines of communication open.

There is an old Native American saying, *"The Great Spirit gave you two ears and only one mouth, so you can talk half as much as you listen."* You must remain willing to listen as well as talk, even when what you are being told about yourself is hard to accept. Don't judge, get angry, or instantly assume that what your partner is telling you about yourself isn't, to some degree, true. If you share this opportunity without lashing out, you may find out that the reason your relationship is failing is resulting from your own misinterpretation of your partner's feelings and actions. Which are in essence simply assumptions that you have made.

Unfortunately, dreams and desires are not all we attempt to hide from each other. Attitudes and personality traits are often hidden in the beginning as well, and these are equally as important. Acceptance is so important in keeping a relationship moving in a positive direction. As I stated earlier, a lot of relationships fail when things about your partner, that never bothered you before, later begin to bother you. You must continually evaluate your relationship, observing not only every existing dimension, but every developing dimension of the person opposite you. You must frequently express what you admire, or very gently point out things that truly bother you. Remember, this is a two-way street, and neither of you is perfect, so be prepared to listen as well as talk. The alternatives - demanding changes while refusing to compromise, constant fighting, and withdrawal from each other - are not beneficial to any relationship.

"It is a great thing to know your vices."
Cicero

Although no one ever achieves perfection, the objective in the pursuit of a healthy relationship is harmony and balance. Effective listening provides an understanding of the overall person, as well as his or her needs, once the façade we often hide behind during the initial romance is removed. Identify what aspects of your partner balance you, and what parts of you balance him or her. This harmony, this interdependence you create, is the key to achieving this. Undoubtedly, interdependence is more easily achieved through expectancy than through expectation.

> **"Life is like riding a bicycle. To keep
> your balance you must keep moving."**
> *Albert Einstein*

If, however, your relationship is very one-sided, if you mistakenly placed a halo over your partner based on false expectations, you may never experience a level of honesty in your relationship. While it is painful to acknowledge that a person may not be truly right for you, staying in a relationship and moving forward with someone you feel you can't talk to or someone you may grow to dislike is, at the very least, counterproductive.

For this reason it is important to remain open minded, and be willing to invest the time to learn from, and to understand each other more. You should try to discover something new, with or about your partner, as often as possible. Just imagine how much more fun your relationship can be everyday if these discoveries take place with open minds instead of with expectations! There really are no limits to where a relationship can take you if you share the journey together.

> **"Don't tell me the sky's the limit when
> there are footprints on the moon."**
> *Paul Brandt*

Unfortunately, however, it is human nature to allow ourselves to believe that our relationships reach a point where they hold no new adventure for us. This is usually when a lot of us decide to "take time apart" and step away from a relationship. We believe, somehow, that this will help to restore the relationship; to take a vacation from each other so to speak. A vacation is defined as "a time devoted to pleasure, rest and relaxation, generally time away from work or school, and taken together as a family unit." How can a relationship succeed if you need to take a vacation from each other, not with each other? Doesn't this signal that the relationship is just too much work and that it provides little reward or pleasure? More often than not, this is when people allow outside influences, or new relationships, to bring about the beginning of the end, instead of a new beginning, to many relationships.

In this stage of your relationship, you may be feeling that you do not have enough in common to make the relationship succeed long term. Before you approach your partner, make a list of your hopes and dreams. By that I mean do you desire to further your education, see yourself changing careers, or engaging in new hobbies? Ask your partner then to make a similar list for their self. Then together make a game of sharing these with each other by guessing each other's answers. You can ask your partner, for example, "Which of these do you think I would most likely try: dancing, bungee jumping, running a marathon?" You may be surprised what you can learn about your partner if you approach this in a fun way together. You may even be surprised to find out how much they actually know about you, and that you may even share similar desires and interests!

Identity

***Phase 3: You develop a unique relationship
based upon your intimate discoveries.***

If you have made it to this phase, *congratulations!* You are now ready to set sail for that imperfectly perfect destination that is life and love! This is often described as the phase where you make the decision to stay in the relationship or end it. I feel that this decision should have already been made in the Understanding Phase; the phase of learning as much as possible about each other, of discovering who each of you truly is.

The Identity Phase is where I propose that you now begin to look ahead and begin to prepare your relationship for a lifetime together. Now is the time to take your lives from *you and me,* to "*we*" -- a shared identity. An identity that is an assemblage of two individual sets of dreams, desires, hopes, strengths, weaknesses, character, flaws, and personalities. A philosophical definition of identity is *"sameness, or whatever makes an entity (we) definable and recognizable."* Ultimately you are striving, not only to develop your relationship, but also to create a lasting, supportive partnership.

**"Love does not consist in gazing at each
other, but in looking outward together
in the same direction."**
Antoine de Saint-Exupery

Your relationship identity should become an inseparable bond. If your partnership is solid, then nothing can break that bond. It is important, however, that you always remember that this shared identity does come from two individual identities. You must be careful to continue to nurture and encourage each other to grow, and not settle into a routine of expectations. Above all, be proud of and appreciate those unique gifts that set you apart! By learning to employ interdependence through expectancy, you are really celebrating these differences by discovering together how these qualities enhance and unite the two of you. Ultimately helping the two of you achieve your goals and dreams together.

"It costs nothing to dream and everything not to."
Rodney White

This breeds hope that the relationship can continue to grow, change, and become even more beautiful and exciting over time. The differences between you are equally a part of your new shared identity, even if not prominently displayed to others. The Identity Phase on the compass moves the direction of the relationship from Encouraging to Nurturing.

Just as every person has an identity, so does a relationship. Have you ever heard your friends referring to others as *"that happy couple,"* or *"that mismatched pair, how did they ever wind up together?"* These are labels that are being placed upon relationships by outsiders, based solely upon their external observations. From these two observations, one would first "expect" that *"the happy couple"* is a match made in heaven. Two scenarios exist for this: one, they truly are a perfect match, or two, they have created a facade for others to see. For the *"mismatched pair,"* similar scenarios exist. Quite often, though, what others see is not always what is real. If the identity you create together is based on expectancy, what you truly are together will be evident to others. The foundation of the identity you develop will be based on the amount of Encouraging and Nurturing you are willing to give to it.

"I know there is strength in the
differences between us. I know
there is comfort where we overlap."
Ani DeFranco

In this stage you, or your partner, may start to feel that your individual identity has been overshadowed by your relationship. Before you allow this feeling to breed discontent in your relationship, try this exercise. Together, make a list of things that you believe identify you to the outside as a "team." Then list what each of you contributes to that identity. Look at how that identity would disappear without both contributions. Let's say, for example, that you built a business together. One of you may have a creative or technical expertise, while the other the skill to manage and market the business. Generally the one considered to be the more clerical is overshadowed by the one with the creativity or expertise. Both roles in this scenario are significant, and recognizing this together helps to solidify this bond you share with pride. Once you've identified to each other how significant a role each of you plays in the union, it will strengthen your relationship. You may even find yourself praising your partner to others for what strengths they bring to the relationship.

Diversity

Phase 4: This is when you learn to accept each other by discovering solutions to your differences.

This is, perhaps, the most important stage of your relationship. It sets the tone for your future together. You have set sail on this beautiful journey together and you have merged into that one, beautiful state of being that is "we." As we continue to grow together, however, our differences, our unexpressed dreams, can once again fragment into pieces of individual identity that we may be reluctant to share. Some of us call this a mid-life crisis. While you have now achieved a level of acceptance of each other, the "me" inside of the "we" may be calling out for yet another change.

"It is the things in common that make a relationship enjoyable, but it is the little differences that make them interesting."
Todd Ruthmann

We have acknowledged that change is inevitable. We must be willing to embrace it, but above all, we must be willing to share it. Change in you may not always be apparent to your partner, or you may in fact be hiding it. Often when change is not understood, as I've stated before, it becomes a reason to accuse. For instance, both women and men, as they age, want to recapture something: youth perhaps, or a desire to feel attractive to others. Often, this becomes cause to accuse your partner of looking for something, or someone, new. Or, as is often the case, we feel a need to explore a part of our self that

101

we may have newly discovered. Or something we may not have ever shared before: a love of singing, a desire to write or paint. The partner who is most content with things as they are can perceive this as a desire to move in another direction, usually away from him or her. This perception, this expectation of failure, can be avoided by embracing change and communicating with expectancy. Let's say that one partner secretly submitted a work of fiction to a magazine and it was published. The appropriate reaction of the other partner should be "Wow, I am so proud of you, are you going to submit more work?" Instead of being met with suspicion or anger, "Why did you do this without telling me?"

Some other differences we may encounter in our relationships are often cultural in nature. Earlier, in Chapter One, I referenced the story of my first encounter, as a young child, with society's inability to embrace diversity. Society has taught us to become close-minded, causing us often to judge others based on predetermined, biased expectations, even before we get to know them. Thankfully, today things are beginning to change. Over the last twenty years or so society has begun to change how it views differences in our relationships. For example, through marriage, we have now crossed cultural borders that once were cause for anger and fear. This, though, presents new challenges that you will need to overcome. When you and your partner come from different ethnic backgrounds, for example, you may experience from, or project onto, your partner, a reluctance to accept things you don't understand. Particularly those things involving family traditions or religious ceremonies. Diversity requires tolerance, understanding, and acceptance. Diversity on the compass moves the relationship from Encouraging to Working together.

Diversity is a very big part of life and relationships. It is not just a mixing of cultures and traditions, or just having different dreams or desires at the onset of the relationship. Every individual is unique and possesses many different characteristics and dimensions. Some of which may come to the surface at different times throughout a relationship. If you see a metamorphosis occurring in your partner, never expect the worst. Instead, with expectancy, praise the other for the changes that you see blossoming right in front of you. Never assume the direction you are headed cannot be changed, even if you are feeling that you are on opposite courses. Changes are not differences. If you truly support your partner, and he or she truly supports you, you will be able to work together in the relationship. You may both see that there can be no limit to the destinations and adventures that lie ahead.

For this stage, take a little time to list all of the characteristics that make your partner both exciting and unique to you. When you have each finished read them aloud to each other. It may surprise you to find out that your partner is drawn to a number of things about you that you might not have been aware of. Remember, quite often it is the things that set you apart from each other that can actually help reignite the passion in your relationship. Especially, when you discover these differences may have been what united you in the first place!

Experience

Phase 5: The desire to expand and improve your relationship is based on growing knowledge.

The fifth, and most enduring, stage of your beautiful journey together is experience. If your relationship is based on expectancy, this is when you realize that the one you are with is the one who truly puts the wind in your sails. This is where you begin to cherish the person you have chosen to share your life with. This is the treasure you have been seeking. This is the couple that grows old together, and still walks together holding hands, but this is not where the story ends.

Treasure is defined as *"something that is highly valued."* More often than not, we do not place enough value on relationships to consider them treasures. Especially, if we have set an expectation for our relationship that "This is all it will ever be." One common definition for a relationship is *"an association or connection between two parties."* Not much romance in *that* definition! Even *romance* provides a better definition for a relationship; *"an ardent emotional attachment or involvement between people."* One can see that an ardent emotional attachment could be considered a treasure, but an association or connection is far less romantic. So, I'll stop trying to rewrite the dictionary, and just propose this: just as gold is, just as silver is, just as diamonds are, a relationship is a treasure.

When we find treasure, our primary objective is to shine it up and display it, with expectancy that it will invite admiration. Why, then, do we not do this with our relationships? We never throw out treasure because it is worn with age. That makes it *more* valuable, and gives us more reason to restore the beauty. Unfortunately, many people only see relationships as connections that can be easily broken and discarded, instead of restored. This is due to a common cultural expectation that most relationships will eventually fail. Until we learn to consider our relationships to be treasures, we will never work to restore them, to bring the shine back!

While, like a treasure, a relationship can age, the hearts and minds of the partners never do. Take time with each other, and if you haven't already expressed the desire to learn and do new things together, do it now! Expanding your knowledge together is to expand your experiences. I'm not saying that you are necessarily in your twilight years when you reach this stage in your relationship; you may only be thirty or forty. Refusal, however, at any point in the relationship to try new things together, or to share new experiences, is to stop working together, to stop dreaming, and ultimately, to lose hope.

"Twenty years from now you will be more disappointed by the things that you didn't do than by the ones you did. So throw off the bowlines. Sail away from the safe harbor. Catch the trade winds in your sails. Explore. Dream. Discover."
Mark Twain

For a relationship to thrive it needs to remain inspired. Don't lose sight of where you and your partner are, as my wife and I did. Love is never automatic; it requires both hope and work to succeed. Failure, a commonly shared expectation, does not have to be an inevitable consequence of love. It only takes nurturing, sharing, encouraging, and working together to achieve success.

For this final stage, make a list of things your partner has expressed interest in trying or accomplishing. Look at these things and identify ways you can support and participate in them. When you have finished, share the lists you have made with each other. Find out how much your partner knows about your interests and how much you know about his or hers. It is also exciting to discover that you may have some new interests in common.

After you complete the *G.U.I.D.E.* on the next two pages, you will greatly improve your understanding of your relationship. It may even provide you with direction to achieve a fresh start, as many times as you need one!

**"The secret to a rich life is to have
more beginnings than endings."**
Dave Weinbaum

The G.U.I.D.E.

1) <u>GROWTH</u> – Invite your partner on a new "first date." Discuss your initial attraction and your hopes for the relationship. Briefly summarize the encounter and your new first impression (see page 88).

_____

_____

_____

_____

_____

_____

2) <u>UNDERSTANDING</u> – List 3-5 things you haven't done before that you would like to try or accomplish. Have your partner do the same. Take turns guessing what your partner's dreams are based on how well you know them or think you know them (see page 96).

_____

_____

_____

_____

_____

_____

3) <u>IDENTITY</u> – List 3-5 things that identify you as a team to the outside, to your family and friends. Then identify your individual contribution to those efforts (see page 99).

_____

_____

_____

_____

_____

_____

4) <u>DIVERSITY</u> – List all the characteristics that you see in your partner that make them exciting and unique to you. Share them with each other to discover how you feel about each other (see page 103)

_____

_____

_____

_____

_____

_____

5) <u>EXPERIENCE</u> – List as many things as you can that your partner has expressed interest in. Share them with each other to see how much your partner knows of your interests and you of his or hers. (see page 107)

_____

_____

_____

_____

_____

_____

CHAPTER FOUR

Let's Get S.M.A.R.T.

"All intelligent thoughts have already been
thought; what is necessary is only to try
to think them again."
Johann Wolfgang von Goethe

- Chapter Four -

I have come to realize that there is a lot of talk and theory about how, why, and when relationships fail. Expectations, not surprisingly, are often set for us by so-called "relationship experts." We are instructed to watch for certain "signs" and if we see them in our partner, or our relationship, it is likely to end. They remove expectancy, or hope of success, and replace it with an expectation of failure. Whether intentional or not, they fuel us with reasons to abandon our relationships instead of putting forth the extra effort to change the direction they are heading.

Despite all the theories, advice, and suggestions out there to prevent it, we generally want to believe that failure, if it occurs, results from the actions of our partner. That person we placed the halo above, and not our self. Any advice we may have been provided to encourage us to stay together is often disregarded for a couple of reasons: first, we don't want to work at our relationships, and second, we often refuse to acknowledge that we may even be a part of the problem. We inherently choose to assume that the other party in a relationship, any relationship, is supposed to come to us if there is a problem.

Initially, as my relationship fell into decline, I had the expectation that everything that was wrong in my relationship was my wife's fault. I believed I had no hand in the impending failure, I believed she pulled away from me. Ironic, that even though I spent the last five years as a college instructor, teaching others how to effectively communicate, I sat back and watched my marriage fall apart due to (pardon this over utilized cliché) *"a failure to communicate."* I didn't see it coming!

Instead of talking, or listening to my wife, I just sat idly by waiting for her to communicate with me. Through most of this bleak period in my life, I did as most people do, I blamed. I blamed my wife for causing our marriage to fail by not openly communicating with me. During the ensuing self-pity, I spent some time soul-searching the possible reasons for *her* failure, still not seeing my own role in all of this. I was, after all, a good provider, in my early forties, still taking great care of my appearance --ok a smidgen vain perhaps--and I believed that I was a pretty good catch. What reason on *Earth* did she have to stop loving me? *What* was not to love?

"Whatever one of us blames in another, each one will find in his own heart."
Lucius Annaeus Seneca

I avoided all of the early signs, her withdrawal from me which in turn caused our physical relationship to deteriorate, her avoidance of being home, lack of any relevant conversations, the list goes on. I did what nearly everyone does when someone they love withdraws from them, as I said before, I blamed. When I finally brushed aside my own bruised feelings I took a long hard look at myself, and where I might have gone wrong. I embarked on this journey, sadly in hindsight, to discover what I might have done when the warning signs manifested.

By failing to communicate effectively with each other, we allow ignorance to become indifference. We do nothing to seek out and repair the minor cracks until it is too late. We have been sailing throughout our lives with a broken compass, with no way to guide our relationship. Essentially, without any real way to find the treasure we all seek – a life shared together in a loving and happy relationship.

In Chapter One I gave an overview of the Halo Effect and how it affects both our relationships, and the way we communicate within those relationships. Before we place that halo over another person, we should look a little deeper inside ourselves. In order to do this it is imperative that we are self-aware of our own strengths and weaknesses. We must be able to analyze our own motivations and feelings, as well as how we act upon them. When I first began to look at how we can communicate more effectively in our relationships, I looked at Emotional Intelligence as a major component of communication.

Emotional Intelligence, as I stated earlier, is a popular and well established concept. It has often demonstrated itself to be more a subjective measurement of conformity than a natural ability, with results that can be more easily faked. This is due to the fact that Emotional Intelligence is deeply rooted in how we respond to others based on how our expectations make us feel, as the concept of expectancy is still in its infancy. Emotional Intelligence is more a method of educating us how to gauge and control emotion, but not how to effectively communicate our true feelings. We are taught how, when our expectations are not met, to control our anger and frustration. We are not taught, however, how these negative feelings might be avoided through expectancy. Emotions are involuntary actions and reactions, coming from our hearts and our heads that do not allow us to see each other for who we truly are. It is reasonable then, to assume that if you are only controlling your emotions some meaning is not getting properly communicated -- that is, something gets lost in translation.

I also shared in Chapter One, that one of the more widely taught components of Emotional Intelligence is Conflict Management. We are told over and over by scientists, scholars, doctors, psychologists, even laymen, that we need to understand the constraints that conflict places on our communication. We are told that we need to identify and understand our "Conflict Style." As I began to peer inward, to view my own relationship from the outside, I realized that it is important not to associate yourself with a communication or conflict style. Styles are ever-changing and, like clothing, you don't want to wear the same thing year after year. Even to understand and identify your style does not mean that its use is appropriate. So I began the process of cleaning out my closet, searching for a means of communicating our emotions to each other, in a decidedly more appropriate fashion.

I concluded that Communication Intelligence was the missing toolkit, comprised of the compass, the inventory, and the guide, all necessary to aid Emotional Intelligence in more effective communication. Tools to be used not just for understanding and managing your emotions, but by using them to communicate with expectancy, learn to guide our emotions instead of just attempting to gauge or control them. Communication Intelligence allows you to respond based on where you hope to be going with your partner if your relationship appears to be going off course. Emotional Intelligence is effective in teaching us to control strong emotional responses to situations based on expectations that, most often, have been set for us by others. Alone, it does not always help us to express hope for a better outcome. Emotions, especially those strong, negative ones, are mostly reactions resulting from past actions and reactions. Harnessing Communication Intelligence allows us to work positively through issues and take a new course rather than repeat bad behaviors, or assume that they cannot be changed.

I've developed Communication Intelligence to help you learn to use effective, expressive language, and honest non-verbal cues, based on expectancy versus expectation in your relationship. Unfortunately, without this insight, I took deliberate, inconsiderate actions towards my wife with an expectation that they would eventually make her "come around." I was wrong. As I continue to detail my experience for you, I hope to open your eyes to the beautiful horizons that await you, if you are willing to open your hearts and truly listen to those closest to you.

> **"The biggest mistake is believing there is one right way to listen, to talk, to have a conversation – or a relationship."**
> *Deborah Tannen*

If you conduct a search on *Communication Intelligence* you will see that the term is associated most often with *S*urveying, *M*apping, *A*nalyzing, *R*esearch, and *T*ransition, in a context of national security, business, and technological advances. I theorized that all of these terms would fit, albeit somewhat abstractly, into an interpersonal perspective. What I discovered, during this compilation, was that all of these terms are just as meaningful and applicable to human interaction -- to relationships -- based on expectancy. I arrived at true Communication Intelligence, of being *S.M.A.R.T.*, and how to apply it to our relationships.

Surveying

"To examine as to condition, situation or value."

Today, we are usually only willing to survey the condition of our relationship in an effort to ascertain whether or not it continues to have value to us. We are less willing to survey the relationship in depth, to identify the situations or expectations that led to its current condition. We do not take the time to understand where we are, and what we can do to improve the overall health and direction of the relationship.

Taking the time to survey a relationship, rather than basing your decisions on predetermined expectations, allows you to remain objective. It allows you to see things from a different perspective, with hope -- a neutral approach. If you enter into a relationship based on only your first impression, you will undoubtedly end up dissatisfied. To survey your relationship is simple. If you believe an issue exists, you just ask questions. Acknowledging that there are no stupid questions, only those that are not asked!

I am endlessly amused by the masses of relationship surveys in magazines and online. These are *not* the tools that will get you the answers you seek. These are generalized surveys that lump all behavior into categories, and "warn" you, with flawed logic, that you should "get out" while you still can! Also, because you complete these surveys based on only your side of the story, the results have no level of accuracy. They only take into account the decisions made by an individual, based often on false assumptions of the partner's actions, that greatly influence those decisions. It is important that the survey you conduct not be an inquisition, a demand for answers. The questions should be carefully worded to elicit honest responses, not defensive reactions.

"Know how to listen, and you will profit even from those who talk badly."
Plutarch

Before you begin to survey, you must first understand that when someone begins to pull away in a relationship, something is happening to him or her. It may be a financial burden he or she is trying to shield you from. Perhaps it is an issue in your partner's outside environment, work or school. Or it may, in fact, be something to do with you or your intimate relationship. There is a very short, simple question to deal with this observed behavior and initiate the survey, and it is *"Please, can we talk?"*

The beauty of using the word please is that it is a caring term, a perfect demonstration of expectancy. It implies that you are willing to listen openly, and navigate past any obstacle in your relationship. It even implies that you are willing to start again. It indicates to your partner that you recognize a need to talk, to work together, and that the conversation will likely not be negative or condescending. Most people understand the value of using the word please, but for those of you who are chuckling over this one take it from me, begin a conversation with *"We* need to talk." and you'll most likely see a defensive reaction. That is because conversations that begin this way are typically negative based on expectations by you of what your partner might have to say.

It is possible that your journey did not begin on the right course, and that the direction you took in the beginning was wrong, but that does not necessarily make failure inevitable. Stop here, ask honest questions of your partner, evaluate the observations you make, and identify the course you are on. If you are headed off course it may be possible to remap your journey, going forward without revisiting any wrong turns you've made along the way.

"The only real mistake is the one from which we learn nothing."
John Powell

Mapping

"A transformation taking the points of one space into the points of the same or another space."

In cartography (map making) to *project* is to transfer features from a spherical surface, such as the earth, to a projection (flat) surface. Inevitably distortion, a false representation of angles and distance, occurs, as it is not feasible to perfectly convert features from an irregular surface to a flat one.

Apply this concept to relationships and what happens is much like that in Columbus's time when people believed that the world was totally flat. They believed that if you sailed too far you just fell off the edge. Similarly, we believe that our relationships are like a straight line. We expect that we can only go so far and our only option is to reverse or we fall off. Moreover, like a number line, if one person reverses, then you move apart. If you both reverse then it feels as though you are taking negative steps backward. When we fail to look at our relationships with hope, as a journey of opportunities, where there are many paths, and many different directions we can travel together, that distortion occurs. We must remember, as I stated in the *G.U.I.D.E.,* every phase we go through in our relationships, just as Columbus ultimately discovered of the earth, takes us in a full circle.

⊢————————————————————————⊣

**"By prevailing over all obstacles and
distractions, one may unfailingly arrive
at his chosen goal or destination."**
Christopher Columbus

⊢————————————————————————⊣

How do we identify the direction we should be taking? Just as you must make sure the points on a map are credible before you begin a journey, our behaviors and actions must be just as credible. Just as forces of nature, earthquakes and tsunamis can alter a terrain and require revisions to a map, our behaviors and actions can change and we may need to alter them as well. If you have taken the initial step, that *"please, can we talk"* moment, you may have only touched on one small issue, or point, on the changing map of your relationship.

One conversation does not necessarily mean that a problem has been resolved. Nor does it mean that only one problem existed in your relationship. You must study the impact that the past behaviors, the forces so to speak, have inflicted on your relationship. You must identify how they have altered the terrain, to see what changes are evident in the relationship. If the map needs a lot of revision, one conversation may not make all things better and another, maybe more, may be needed.

When someone is withdrawing and holding back, you must understand that there may also be a fear of total disclosure based on an expectation of anger or rejection. Especially, if the reason the person is holding back is based on past issues in communicating with you; fighting and distrust, for example. Generally, when someone avoids asking what is wrong, it is evident that he or she would much rather avoid the issue, or worse, blame and make accusations, often causing the other partner to withdraw even further. As often as you can, take a step back and communicate with yourself before communicating with your partner. Ask yourself if you have always been honest about your fears, your insecurities, or even, well what we have been talking about since the beginning of this book, your refusal to accept any responsibility for the changing terrain.

**"Map out your future – but do it in pencil.
The road ahead is as long as you make it.
Make it worth the trip."**
Jon Bon Jovi

It is your willingness to initiate a dialogue with your partner that will help him or her really see that things are not as hopeless as they may have believed. The course of your life may require some remapping and you must be willing to explore that process. *"Please, let me help* ~~you~~ *(strike that!)* <u>us</u> *work through this."* "Please" really *is* the most forgotten word in the English language, especially where relationships are concerned. Perhaps the second most forgotten is "us."

Analyzing

*"To resolve anything complex
into its elements."*

You must be able to identify the elements that hold your relationship together. It is true, you sometimes feel like you must be a Rocket Scientist to understand the complexity of relationships. Let us just continue on this journey that is our relationship, and I'll share more of what I learned about communicating with each other, to keep us going in the same direction.

Think you don't have to analyze your relationship? Wrong, you do, but as everyone knows you can over-analyze anything. The trick is finding out how to analyze the needs you both have, and not just the present state of your relationship, or even how you got there. Before we can begin to understand our relationship, we must first decide what our relationship is based on. The tendency we have when we begin a new relationship is to determine the investment we will be making, and what return we are looking for in that investment based on our expectation of success or failure.

Much as we do with our financial investments, we seek out relationships based on the maximum return we expect from them. More often than not, we fall into the aggressive, short-term investment strategy. That is, when we feel that there is no longer any value to be obtained, and we have depleted the resources in our portfolio, it is time to invest in something new. This is often when we are more likely to pull out of our relationship, and invest in a new relationship that provides us with instant reward and gratification.

This value-based, cultural perspective only serves to sabotage our relationships. When you start a business, you invest what you have into seeing that business succeed: time, money and passion. If we believe in the business, and in what we are doing, we will continue to invest during economic slowdowns. We do this because we know that the additional investment may cost us a little more in the short run, but will ultimately pay off in the long run. Also, by continuing to invest, we don't risk losing everything. This hope, or belief in a positive outcome, drives our success. We do not set an expectation of failure. Isn't it funny that we can look at business, but not at our relationships this way? In our relationships, we tend to see too many other options available to us. We fail to see value in the long term investment. We accept challenge in business, but not in love.

Consider also the financial impact of a failed short-term investment. So much money and time is wasted when we choose to invest in a new relationship, rather than maintain, or re-invest in our existing one. Lawyers, support, maintenance of two households instead of one, the list goes on. We need to stop viewing our relationships with this emotionally charged investment strategy, and learn to explore all the new opportunities that await us. My twenty year investment ended without the return I had hoped for.

"Love is grand; divorce is a hundred grand."
Anonymous

While teaching *Success Strategies*, a college course developed by Skip Downing, I discovered some interesting insight into why this "quick return" mindset may plague our relationships. In his book *On Course:*

Strategies for Creating Success in College and in Life he cites a 1960's experiment conducted on four year old children in a preschool. In this experiment, the children were offered one marshmallow immediately, or two if they would wait for 20 minutes, in an effort to determine which children were emotionally charged (seeking instant gratification) and which were emotionally intelligent (willing to endure some discomfort for a greater reward.) The study went on to conclude that those who were willing to wait for the greater reward, who demonstrated emotional control, went on to achieve greater success in life.

Based on the alarmingly high divorce rates today, this signifies to me that most relationships are emotionally charged. We will not likely achieve success in our relationships until we accept that there will be some discomfort at times. We need to recognize that we must work for the reward, often involving waiting or riding out the tough times together, if we want our relationships to succeed. This can be more easily achieved if we integrate Communication Intelligence with Emotional Intelligence.

It is said that unlike almost everything else we do in life, with communication, once something is done it cannot be undone. You cannot truly take back what has been said. As I have stated before, it is best to move away from analyzing what you said or did to bring you to the present state and focus on using **A.R.E. Language**, defined in Chapter Two, to seek a better outcome.

**"Water and words.
Easy to pour impossible to recover."**
Zen Proverb

It is equally important that you also take the responsibility of analyzing what your own internal needs, dreams, and desires are, and then openly share them with your partner. This open sharing between you ensures that this investment you have in each other continues to increase in value. You may actually find that there are many similarities in what you both hope to gain from the relationship.

Never begin this sharing with "When we first met *you*...." or the analysis stops and the walls go up. This "you" statement can be perceived as a "warning shot across the bow." It implies that you blame your partner. That somehow "*you* have grown to disappoint *me*" based on an expectation you may have set for your partner. We should never use "you" statements in our conversations. "Remember when *we* first met, how *we* used to..." is a much better way to begin to analyze using Communication Intelligence. The "we" statement more appropriately identifies your dreams and desires by referring to a shared passion, or action that may have been lost along the way, one that you hope to recover. It does not focus on what you are doing individually, but on how you hope to reconnect. It also expresses a true desire to analyze when, again not how, the journey took a wrong turn and asks, "How do we return to that place where we were happy?" The reaction you receive to the second statement will more likely meet the expectancy you seek.

"Then Jesus touched their eyes and said, Let it happen, then, just as you believe."
Matthew 9:29 (GNT)

Research

*"Systematic exploration conducted
to gain knowledge."*

Is there any more beautiful aim than continuing to explore a relationship? To explore is to be willing to continuously learn from each other, and about each other. Here is where you develop a system, based on your ability to analyze, to survey, and to find the points on your map. You both must be willing to open up with expectancy, and honestly share those things you might have been inclined to hold back based on negative expectations.

Desires and fantasies, both beautiful and sensual experiences, if not shared with each other can often become the cause of dissatisfaction in relationships. Generally they become a reason one partner withdraws from the other. This happens when these unshared desires create a longing in one partner that often results in that partner looking outside the relationship for what he or she feels is lacking in the relationship. You are initially attracted to your partner based on some desire or fantasy you project on them in the beginning. If you never share that openly with each other, when one partner feels that the other has failed to live up to their expectations, he or she is no longer satisfied.

You should never give up researching and exploring each other's desires. This can be done by initiating conversations using simple romantic statements. *"You are still my Prince Charming."* serves to let a man know that his partner senses a strong fantasy side to him and he should play off of that. *"You were and still are the most beautiful woman I've ever seen."* after any number of years of marriage, shows a woman his romantic side. While conversations generated by these statements may ultimately end up with you watching an inordinate amount of "chick flicks" with your partner, it can lead to many benefits, not the least of them being renewed passion!

"In the end, it's not going to matter how many breaths you took, but how many moments took your breath away."
Shing Xiong

Another aspect of research, often overlooked in relationships, is to propose new activities, to encourage each other to try new things together. I am not talking about jumping from planes, or deep sea diving, unless that is your cup of tea. I'm saying you should seriously look at things you currently both enjoy doing. Then do some research and seek out different activities that complement those interests. For example, if you like to go to clubs to dance, then suggest taking ballroom dance lessons together. If you like watching home improvement shows, try a day out visiting model homes, to view firsthand the latest building and decorating trends. If you love watching singing talent shows on television, go out and try karaoke together. Subtle deviations in your normal routines may open you up to new interests, new experiences. As detailed in Chapter 3, Experience is the most rewarding phase of your relationship, because when driven by expectancy, it brings the relationship around full circle. New experiences bring new beginnings, new growth. Never stop exploring new opportunities to learn and share things together. To continue to try new things together keeps your relationship inspired. It means that you will never stop dreaming!

"The more connections you and your lover make, not just between your bodies, but between your minds, your hearts, and your souls, the more you will strengthen the fabric of your relationship, and the more real moments you will experience together."
Barbara De Angelis

Transition

"The act of passing from one state or place to the next".

Understanding that people and relationships are ever changing, it is still human nature to want to cling to that elusive moment when we meet for the first time. That desire we felt that took our breath away. To that undeniable chemistry that attracts us to one another...to romance...to magic!

**"Love and magic have a great deal in common.
They enrich the soul, delight the heart.
And they both take practice."**
Unknown

When first felt, it seems as if nothing could ever change that fairytale moment...that expectation that what we are experiencing in that moment will last forever. Eventually, though, it does change and daily life comes into focus. When that happens, we tend to use the expression *"The honeymoon is over."* This is often when our initial expectation for the relationship is not met and dissatisfaction sets in.

To clarify, the term *"honeymoon"* is not exactly as romantic as one might think. Folklore has it that the expression originated over 4000 years ago in Babylon, when for a full month after the wedding the bride's father would supply his new son-in-law with all the honey-beer he could drink. Leading one to pose the question, "What was wrong with his daughter?"

Honeymoon is, in fact, a fairly accurate representation of what we expect from our relationships. To remain drunk with ecstasy and passion that will transcend time, but that is not reality. Reality is that every relationship undergoes numerous transitions throughout its lifetime, and we must learn to embrace them with expectancy, rather than fear or by ignoring them.

"Things do not change, we change."
Henry David Thoreau

I ignored the transitions in my own relationship, as most people do. I failed to continue in the ongoing process of researching, of exploring my wife's needs and desires, and of sharing my own. I avoided the processes of surveying, and analyzing the changes in the attitudes and behaviors in both of us. I failed to observe the course my relationship was taking, until it was too late to remap the journey. In essence, I was not *S.M.A.R.T.!*

I hope you are beginning to see that all of these things are not just about how you communicate verbally, but how critical all of your non-verbal actions are to the relationship as well.

CHAPTER FIVE

F.I.N.D. Out Where You Need to Be

"Happiness is a direction,

not a place."

Sydney J. Harris

- Chapter Five -

The indicator needle on a compass is the feature that allows you to *F.I.N.D.* out where you are. In sailing, as you change direction you keep an eye on the compass needle, to make sure the turn you take is heading you in the right direction. You must *F.I.N.D.* out where you are before you know where you are going.

This chapter focuses on the importance of nurturing, so that the decisions you make in your relationship, especially the decision to stay in it and grow it, are based on *F*acts, *I*nitiative, *N*eed, and *D*edication. It is impossible to grow something without knowing the facts about it. Facts are not expectations; however, knowing the facts *can* promote expectancy. Plants, for example, require you to know whether they thrive in sunlight or in shade, whether they need lots of water or are drought resistant, and what seasons they will grow in. You must have the initiative to find out the facts, as these facts identify the needs the plant has for growth. You must also determine whether you have the dedication required to nurture the growth. Relationships require much the same nurturing as plants. Before you can nurture growth in a relationship, you must set aside all previous expectations in order to uncover the facts on which the relationship is based. You must have the initiative to determine from those facts what needs the relationship will have, as well as the dedication from both partners, that will be required to grow the relationship.

To find, is by definition, to "come upon or discover by searching or making an effort." What you visualize in the beginning of your relationship has little to do with discovery, and everything to do with appearance, as I've stated numerous times in the previous chapters. The true discovery in any relationship, is finding out all you can about each other, determining if your feelings are mutual, and deciding if this is the person you wish to continue to grow with.

**"The essence of life is finding something
you really love and then making the
daily experience worthwhile."**
Denis Waitley

$\underline{F}_{act}$

"A truth known by actual experience or observation," or alternately, "something said to be true to supposed to have happened."

Before you can nurture a child, you must be able to teach them. To teach, you must be able to seek out the facts. You must do the same before you can nurture a relationship. The most important thing we often fail to do in our relationship is to evaluate what we perceive as *fact*. To ascertain whether what we believe to be fact, is supposed or actual. Many relationships breakup over suppositions: those things we assume to be factual, things that are not yet proven, versus the actual facts. These suppositions are most often derived from the expectations we set for our relationships. Unfortunately, these expectations are generally based on probability rather than on actual facts. When we do this we fail to continuously improve ourselves, and our relationships, by not wanting to pursue a different outcome if the suppositions prove to be true. Instead we jump on this as an opportunity to sabotage, or end the relationship, rather than allow ourselves to be injured by our partner. Obviously, we are not communicating intelligently when we choose to do this!

"Assumptions are the termites of relationships."
Henry Winkler

Worse than assuming unproven things to be facts, we solicit advice from others around us. You will never get unbiased advice or opinions from others unless, of course, you are paying for professional intervention. Typically, with friends and family, we present only one side of an issue – ours -- and naturally, they take our side. Their advice can also present us with "facts" we assume to be true, based on someone else's "similar" experience. Often, however, their experience is altogether different. This goes back to earlier in the book where I explained that often we do not see our self as part of the problem. We do not present both sides of the story in order to obtain objective advice. We allow the expectation of failure to sabotage our relationship because we believe it to simply be "what usually happens."

"Know when to tune out, if you listen to too much advice you may wind up making other peoples mistakes."
Ann Landers

As I explained in Chapter Four, using **S.M.A.R.T.** communication requires that you keep the channels open, and be able to sort through all the useless information retrieved. Especially that offered by those around us, who plant seeds of doubt that we allow to grow like weeds. If we are afraid to ask the questions then we have already accepted the suppositions to be true. We must be willing to seek out the truth. To do this we must talk and be open to whatever the facts are, whether they are true or untrue. More importantly, we must be willing to work with our partner to determine if the facts presented are a strong enough reason to abandon a relationship.

If you are a little lost here, one of the most common scenarios where facts are presented from those outside our relationship involves cheating. What is becoming more and more commonplace today is a new level of cheating described as "emotional cheating." Emotional cheating, considered by some to be harmless, more often than not, ultimately leads to physical cheating. Whether one is engaged in physical cheating, or emotional cheating, with someone outside the relationship it is because they feel something is lacking in their relationship.

I do not condone cheating in any form *–unless it's death or taxes* ☺ -- but I do want others to realize that this is often the end result when partners do not communicate their needs to each other. Take emotional cheating. That is when you share your private, but mostly negative feelings, about your relationship with a co-worker or close or casual friend. Or now, as has become more popular due to internet social mediums, a pen pal or old friend we haven't connected with in a long time. Many people believe this to be harmless chatter, or just releasing frustration with friends, never intentionally setting out to damage their relationship. We often fail to recognize that, in some cases, these friends may have a different agenda than we do, and they themselves may become the source of disclosure for facts that are not true.

Back to Growth, in Chapter 3, I stated that in relationships, we should be friends first. That our partner is the one person we should want to share everything about our relationship with. That is a huge leap of faith for some people. We tend to set an expectation that we cannot discuss the frustrations we have with our partner, *with* our partner, for fear of hurting them. This shuts down an important line of communication: sharing our true feelings with each other. What, and how, we feel about each other are the facts we need to be the most open about to truly keep our relationship growing.

Initiative

"Without prompting or direction from others."

You cannot just sit back and go along for the ride in a relationship. If I have learned anything from my own experience, it is that no one wants to feel like they are the only one in the relationship taking action when things are going wrong. No one wants to feel like they are the only one putting in the effort to keep the excitement, the fire, going.

One does not take initiative without being able to communicate in some form, verbally or non-verbally, to their partner. There is no better demonstration of expectancy in a relationship than taking the initiative to engage your partner. For any relationship to be successful, both partners must be willing to take initiative at times. When one person seems to be exhibiting more initiative than the other, this does not necessarily mean he or she cares about the relationship more than the other partner does. This is a common misinterpretation.

Men most often misinterpret this by assuming that if they are usually the one to initiate intimate relations, that their partner is "not really interested." We have discussed assumptions, those false expectations, a number of times in this book, but this is a common assumption that leads to frustration, as well as a lack of desire to communicate. Women, I've discovered, as it has been repeatedly stated in books and on talk-shows, are wired differently than men. Through societal programming, they are expected to allow men to *make the first move,* so to speak. Men, being wired the way we are, are always looking for excitement. Where does this leave us when we don't communicate? It leaves us making assumptions about what each of us believes our partner feels about the relationship. In this one common scenario, men view the women as uninterested, and women see men as someone likely to cheat on them. Neither is usually true, and you need to learn to talk openly about it. Tell your partner what you want. If you are a man, and it excites you for your partner to "take the lead" at times, share that with her. Explain that in your intimate relations there is no one else there to judge any unconventional behavior. The most important thing to remember is that if you are the one who feels unsatisfied, you must be willing to take the first step and be open and honest with your partner.

Refusing to take initiative because it defies convention, or for fear of rejection, are the most common expectations causing us to hold back from our partner. When we hold back we are not allowing our desires, or our partner's desires, to be satisfied. The more frequently we hold back, the more dissatisfied we become. Don't just take the initiative to be the first one to act, take the initiative to be the first one to start a dialogue. Rest assured you are probably both feeling the same way. Whoever takes the initiative first opens the door to his or her partner to do the same. As I said before, stop waiting each other out to see who goes first.

**"Initiative is doing the right
things without being told."**
Elbert Hubbard

$\underline{\text{N}}$eed

"To want or require something."

Earlier in this book I explained that when we see people in need, we give. Without hesitation, we give our food, our money, even our time, to total strangers, to fill a need they have. Why, then, are we reluctant to identify and satisfy our needs, or the needs of our partner, in our relationship?

There is a wonderful story floating about the internet about a practice started in Naples, Italy some say about a hundred years ago. People who were more fortunate would purchase coffee in shops and while paying for their own, would pay for "suspended" coffees. These suspended coffees would then be made available to the less fortunate when they would come in and ask for them. The practice became more commonplace during World War II. Even today, with so many regions suffering economic collapse, this generosity of spirit, of sharing, has extended to other countries, even the United States.

Similarly, my father, as I was growing up, ran a wonderful deli and used to delight in giving away samples to patrons and passersby, even when they weren't there to make a purchase. He always made a point of giving far more than the expected amount to those who did make purchases. He didn't do it, like the mass marketers of today, giving a little in the hopes of generating bigger sales, he did it because it made him happy, and it made those he shared with happy. He was cultivating relationships, not customers.

For the majority of us who would exhibit this generosity of spirit, we do it without expectation of reward. Most people, I believe, are born with an inherent willingness to share with others, to fulfill their needs, because it makes us feel better about ourselves. Ironically, while we see the needs of those outside our relationships and are inspired to share, we are reluctant to look at the person closest to us to see or understand his or her needs. Which, more often than not, are needs that are not even material in nature.

We all know that love is a powerhouse of emotions. When we believe that we have a need that goes unfulfilled, that our partner has somehow overlooked or is oblivious to, we tend to get selfish. When we hurt inside, we in turn inflict emotional pain on our partner because we have a need that we believe our partner is not willing to satisfy. More often than not, it is not your partner who is failing to recognize and satisfy those needs -- it may be that you have not effectively communicated that need to him or her. You have simply expected that they should somehow know. Some of the most obvious needs in any relationship are: acceptance, forgiveness, intimacy, equality, trust, and respect.

"The best relationship is one in which your love for each other exceeds your need for each other."
Anonymous

If you believe in psychic ability, then you know that those with the ability to read minds are among the few, not the many. Unfortunately, in relationships, while we would truly love to believe in the sentiment that "we are one" - *we are not*! We are still two separate individuals, who likely do not possess the ability to communicate telepathically. If you feel, for example, that any of the needs I listed above are not being satisfied by your partner, then it is time for you to open a dialogue. Usually, however, fear of reprisal or conflict causes us to engage in silly mind games. Very much the opposite of mental telepathy! Mind games are not good games either. They are, essentially, power struggles which serve to demoralize the opponent, and undermine their perceptions.

Pouting is *a mind game*. The statement *"You should have known."* is a mind game *opening strategy*. And restrictions, such as withholding physical intimacy for example, against your opponent for not fulfilling a need he or she *"Should have known."* are *bad moves*! It will, most likely, lead to a guaranteed defeat. Games are more fun when played together, not on each other.

Since it has been said that conflict cannot survive without participation…stop participating. The best way to avoid conflict, or mind games, is to realize that possibly your partner may actually be unaware of the needs you have because you have not shared them. Tell your partner openly what your needs are, and why you feel they are not being met. Don't try to control the dialogue. And don't assume you are the only one who is dissatisfied. Chances are you may be unaware of some of your partner's needs as well. Again, as much as you are prepared to talk, you must be willing to listen.

Dedication

"To be wholly committed to something."

Every job you take requires that you dedicate yourself completely to it in order to achieve maximum success. The more successful we become the bigger the reward, which in the case of a job means a bigger paycheck or a bonus. Similarly, we must be dedicated to nurturing our relationships if we are to succeed in them. Unlike a job, however, in relationship true dedication is a selfless devotion. It is a willingness to cooperate, and care for each other, a promise of loyalty, of faithfulness, and a promise to make each other a priority in the life you share together. Dedication is a trait closely associated with expectancy.

Dedication in a relationship also means that you are willing to stick with each other through good and bad times. Dedication is the willingness to work things out together, instead of laying blame on each other. Dedication is giving it your all, without being prodded or nagged to do so. While dedication is most closely associated with work, nurturing too requires dedication to ensure growth. The dream that nearly everyone shares is to be held closely to someone else's heart, to be loved.

"Dreams and Dedication
are a powerful combination."
William Longwood

Just as dedication to a job sets an expectancy of reward, and makes one less likely to change jobs, dedication in relationships has a similar impact. If we truly give all we have in our relationship to make it succeed, the reward -- true love and happiness -- generally keeps us from seeking change. It keeps us from allowing negative expectations to cause us to give up and seek someone new to fill our needs. My sister Giovanna, who has also dealt with pain in a relationship, shared this profound example of dedication with me; "Never give up hope or give up on people who have hurt you. Hope is the light that leads us out of darkness."

CHAPTER SIX

F.I.S.H. to Survive

"What we see depends mainly
on what we look for."

John Lubbock

- Chapter Six -

This Chapter demonstrates the most fundamental reason we must show our partner our true face. A relationship requires an authentic level of honesty between two people in order to achieve an expectancy of success. Since communication is recognized as being over half non-verbal, the expressions we present must accurately reflect what we are trying to communicate to our partners. Every one of us has feelings we need to acknowledge, and emotions we need to express. Unfortunately, we often hide them behind a mask or facade. Anything less than honest expression, specifically those based on expectations of what we believe we should display, are very often misinterpreted, prompting frustration or avoidance.

When our expressions do not match our words we are often perceived by others as lying. This can be as detrimental to a relationship as telling an actual lie. Worse, by showing non-supportive expressions, you may be unintentionally signaling to your partner that you are no longer interested in him or her. You must learn to put on the face that others hope to honestly see. In this way, expectancy allows us to display our true feelings to our partner without fear of a negative reaction, whereas expectations often cause us to misrepresent ourselves. This is where we need to learn to apply *A.R.E. Language* discussed in Chapter Two.

This chapter defines how non-verbal "language" is crucial to the success of your relationship. To present an honest face, it is imperative that we are able to recognize, and read, our own non-verbal expressions. Since those non-verbal expressions are a manifestation of the emotions we are feeling, delivering the appropriate expressions are important to receiving the desired reactions from our partner.

Communication is an instinctive behavior, necessary for our very survival. We would never consider sending conflicting messages to someone in imminent peril. Using both verbal and non-verbal communication, we would shout out a warning, as well as signaling to the one at risk, of the approaching danger. In relationships we communicate far less effectively, especially when we allow fear or disillusionment to take hold of our relationship. We often find ourselves sending mixed, incomplete, or erroneous messages. These illogically conceived, false expressions only sabotage the credibility we have with our partner.

To survive in relationships we must *F.I.S.H.* for the truth within ourselves, in order to display the truth of our feelings, to our partner. The expressions we most often misrepresent in our relationships are **F**ear, **I**nterest, **S**adness and **H**appiness.

"The longing we have to communicate cleanly and directly with people is always obstructed by qualifications and often with concerns about how our messages will be received."

John Le Carre

Fear

"Something that causes feelings of dread or apprehension; a feeling of anxiety when facing danger."

Fear is probably the most incorrectly expressed emotion in relationships, especially when we are dealing with change. When we fear a violent action or situation, a look of panic, real fear, is an appropriate representation of what we are feeling. The nonverbal expression, however, that typically is reflected in our face when we fear change is disinterest. That is, we tend to appear to barely listen, often while verbally discouraging our partner. This misrepresentation of your true feelings can cause your partner to assume you are not supportive, or that you don't care about them, their interests, or their dreams, thus becoming his or her expectation of how you feel.

If fear is what you feel, then express the honest fear on your face, and most likely, an honest conversation will follow. For instance, if your partner wants to go to college or change careers when you feel like you have provided a life that should have made them happy, you might fear that it is because he or she wants to move away from you. If you say *"I think that's a great idea."* but your face says *"whatever"* it is clear to see that this can be misinterpreted as disinterest. On the other hand, if your face says *"Will you still need me?"* then your partner can sense that your fear is of change, not that you are indifferent to their needs and desires, or unsupportive of their ambitions. If you display this honesty, a dialogue of reassurance for your new future together should follow. This is communicating with expectancy.

159

"Fear is just your feelings asking for a hug."
Unknown

By recognizing what the causes of fear are in ourselves, we are better able to understand our own emotions allowing us to project them correctly. Expectancy provides us the opportunity to share the true expression of our feelings to our partner, instead of controlling or hiding them. Expectancy also allows us to embrace change with enthusiasm and excitement, anticipating that this change, if good for your partner, is also good for the relationship. Nothing brings renewed life to a relationship better than supporting your partner even if you may have some apprehension. Your partner needs the support, because whether you have considered it or not, they are probably just as apprehensive as you. Just knowing that you are in this with them can often eliminate any fear that either of you is experiencing.

Interest

*"A state of curiosity or concern about
or attention to something."*

Interest is another expression we typically do not show to our partner often enough. When your partner engages in something new, something you may not fully understand, you may tend to send out unsupportive signals. I've just discussed how we incorrectly express fear when change is occurring, so now we need to learn to properly show interest by letting go of our ignorance. I do not want to sound redundant here, but ignorance, as with fear, is often expressed as indifference. Ignorance, as an expression, is often referred to as a petulant look. This is an expression of irritability. Have you ever been excited when explaining something to your partner, another family member, or a friend or co-worker, and gotten the response *"Get to the point?"* That is, in its verbal form, petulance. We have all, at some time or another, been given the look that goes with it!

In relationships, we tend to tell our partner that we support them, however when they see this look on your face you are clearly contradicting what your words are saying. If you don't understand what your partner is telling you, or explaining to you, just tilt your head to one side, let your expectations along with indifference fall to the floor, and just listen. You might learn something new. Your ignorance might even be replaced with enthusiasm, and that is an instantly recognizable expression we all like to see on each other's faces! This is communicating with expectancy.

> **"No one cares how much you know, until they know how much you care."**
> *Theodore Roosevelt*

You must always encourage your partner, not only to pursue their interests, dreams, and desires; you must also be willing to share and participate in your most united effort - the relationship. You must continuously encourage your partner to remain committed to the relationship, by being an active participant yourself.

Remember, it is not necessary to have all of the same interests, such as sports, music, reading, etc., but you both must share the same interest in growing the relationship. Don't be ignorant, and avoid change based on negative expectations. Embrace change with expectancy and you may just find out that you and your partner have more in common than you think. Express to your partner, both verbally and non-verbally, that you are willing to take on any new challenge with them.

Sadness

"Affected by unhappiness or grief or sorrow."

People often display, or express, sadness at times when happiness for a friend or partner would be expected. This is due to a negative expectation that if this person achieves a level of success without us, they no longer need us. Often, acknowledging a success or change in one we love causes us to believe we are losing something we thought we had control of. Some of us even choose to grieve the loss of that control. When you exhibit sadness, or worse, channel that sadness into anger, your partner may begin to withdraw from you. Fearing your reaction, this may lead your partner to keep things to his or her self. In other words, it may lead to secrecy. Your partner, wanting to avoid this type of reaction, may choose not to discuss these successes, or changes, with you. Or sadly, in some cases, they may choose to move out of the relationship altogether.

Displaying sadness in lieu of support, in most cases, can lead to angry confrontations. If you understand where your sadness is coming from, take the time to start the conversation with *"Wow, I'm really happy you ..."* followed by *"I need you to know how much I love you, but I need you to help me through this change."* As I have stated all along, it is difficult to control emotions, so putting on a happy face is not always possible. Letting your partner know where the sadness, or anger, is coming from can be far less damaging to a relationship than making your partner feel that they are the cause of your personal unhappiness. By acknowledging your fears, you are expressing to your partner a hope that you can become a part of this change.

I know, from personal experience, that it isn't always easy to recognize where our emotions are coming from. This is the reason I feel it is so important that you allow your partner to share their feelings openly with you, and you with them. Communicating with this level of expectancy shows a strong desire to grow the relationship with your partner, instead of inflicting guilt over your perceived expectation of loss.

"Anger is just a cowardly extension of sadness. It's a lot easier to be angry at someone than it is to tell them you're hurt."
Tom Gates

Happiness

"A state of feeling, showing or expressing joy."

If we are in love we should be happy all the time, right? This is what we are programmed to believe. Unfortunately, for some of us, this is one of those emotional expressions that we reserve for when we are on the receiving end of a gift. How often do we find ourselves smiling at those we love for no reason at all? Believing that just having them with us is a gift.

Have you ever been around a couple where upon when one of them enters a room you instantly see a gleam in the partner's eye? That is expectancy. It is an instinctive reaction that shows the one you love how happy they make you. It is powerful to witness, and a strong indicator that they are engaged in a relationship without any negative expectations of failure. Imagine how it can feel to be a part of a relationship like that! Even one little smile every day, for no reason, can lift not only another's spirit, but your own as well. It lets your partner know that they are appreciated, and that they are loved. This is the face we should put on as much as possible!

**"To love is to place our happiness
in the happiness of another."**
G. Wilhelm Liebniz

Honest expressions often make all the difference in where a conversation starts, or whether one ever begins. Take the time, as I have learned, to listen to what you are saying and reflect what you are saying non-verbally by understanding what your expressions are telling your partner. It is easier than you might think to know what others see. After all, before emotion shows on your face it is felt from the inside. It is not necessary to always try to control your emotions, as long as you are prepared to explain them to your partner. In doing so, you will understand them better yourself. Share your feelings, do not mask, or misrepresent them.

"Now and then it's good to pause in our pursuit of happiness and just be happy."
Guillaume Apollinaire

CHAPTER SEVEN

S.T.O.P. Along the Way

"Love comes when manipulation stops; when you think more about the other person than about his or her reactions to you. When you dare to reveal yourself fully. When you dare to be vulnerable."

Dr. Joyce Brothers

- Chapter 7 -

Non-verbal communication not only affects our relationships, it is an absolutely essential component in building strong relationships. Non-verbal cues can be very different in marriage than when you were dating. While dating, we put up facades, we wear masks to show each other who we want to be, or believe the other wants us to be. This is, very often, not who we truly are. We attempt to hide the bad, based on our expectation of what we believe the other may find unacceptable, and reveal only the good. This hinders us from discovering how the relationship can develop if we display our true character and personality.

As any relationship progresses, despite our best efforts, it becomes extremely difficult to maintain a façade. It is difficult, because the truth eventually seeps through the cracks as they quickly begin to appear. A relationship works best when the facade has a good deal of truth in the design. Even if some elements are only meant to enhance the outward appearance and make it more attractive. People expect flaws, not perfection even when they seek it. People experience disappointment when perfection is falsely displayed. It is very important to the success of any relationship that you represent yourself truthfully to each other. This is indicative of an expectancy of acceptance.

We need to *S.T.O.P.* and show others who we truly are in order to receive the encouragement, and support, we all need to grow as individuals. This does not mean to bring your relationship to a complete stop. More like that of a stop light, than of a stop sign, we need to slow down, be prepared to stop together, and resume once that light has illuminated the best that we both have to share and give. This, in turn, makes our relationships stronger. The personal characteristics that best reflect this level of honesty are: **S**incere, **T**rustworthy, **O**ptimistic and **P**ersistent.

"Three things cannot be long hidden:
the sun, the moon, and the truth."
Buddha

Sincere

"Genuine or real."

Simple enough, right? Teaching college students has allowed me to learn how to read people very well. Observation is essential in teaching. It helps to identify the hidden truths about people. In my experience, for example, a student who is arrogant, professing total understanding of the material, while still failing the course, is often shielding his or her self. The student does not wish to appear to be struggling with the material to the class, or to the instructor. That facade, his or her outward display, is due to anxiety, or fear of rejection or embarrassment. We often put up a façade based on a presumption that others have expectations of who, or what, we should be. Quite often, the facade we display is a polar opposite of who we truly are. This is the defense mechanism we use to shield our self when we are unwilling to admit that we need encouragement and support from others.

"Don't go through life, grow through life."
Eric Butterworth

We all like to present ourselves to others as unique. While in truth, we all are, we still choose to *"make up"* some aspects of who we are to impress others. This is just human nature. If, however, you want a lasting relationship, one that doesn't require apology or explanation later on, you need to take off the mask and be sincere. I know everyone says this, but you have got to accept yourself and just be yourself before you can truly learn to love, and be loved. While the Halo Effect attracts us to what we believe to be true, we are certainly disappointed when we find out it isn't. We love what is real.   Being sincere in our relationship represents expectancy that we will be accepted as we are. In the case of the college student, he might have been surprised by how supportive his classmates would have been if they had sensed he needed help.

We are often our own worst critics, and we set expectations for our self that others do not. Whatever you hide from others you deny to yourself, preventing that person you choose as your life-long partner, from supporting and accepting you for what you truly bring to the relationship. Being sincere with our self, as well as with others, promotes our own self-esteem and in turn allows us to gain so much more from our relationships.

"All you need within you is waiting
to unfold and reveal itself."
Eileen Caddy

Trustworthy

"True, honest and faithful."

Similar to being sincere, others must also be able to trust you. Hiding behind a pretense of who you are is justifiable reason for people you love, not to be able to trust you. Whether it is through actions, expressions, or words, people innately know who they can, and cannot trust. If you want a relationship to remain on course, and you have not been totally honest, you must stop here. In order to establish a relationship that has a foundation of truth, you need to initiate a dialogue and come clean. People in general, especially those who love you, will trust you more if you *"come clean,"* than if you are later *"outed."*

If you are not telling the truth, or only part of the truth, people can tell. If dishonesty is a dominant trait in a person, those closest to them will inevitably form an expectation that nothing in their relationship is based on truth. As I demonstrate to my classes, by showing funny political video clips, you can see when a person's non-verbal expression and reactions are contradicted by what is coming out of their mouth. While humorous to watch, this is not helpful in relationships. Relationships require honesty. To be honest, you must be as trustworthy as you expect your partner to be.

"The best way to find out if you can trust somebody is to trust them."
Ernest Hemingway

While some people are inherently dishonest, others may simply create a pretense of who they are based on an expectation that they don't, in some way, "measure up." Expectancy allows you to accept yourself. It helps you to understand that those who would find you inferior, in some way, are generally hiding behind some pretense of their own. The only person that you can truly know is being honest in a relationship is you. Don't compromise your character to meet someone else's expectation!

"God has given you one face,
and you make yourself another."
William Shakespeare

Optimistic

"Expecting and seeing the best in all things."

It is a tough job, to remain optimistic at all times, and certainly no one is able to do it with 100% success. When you are in a relationship, though, you must try to be as optimistic as possible. Not only when things are going well, but also when things are not at their best. While the halo effect is a bias, an illusion created when one is blind to reality, even if only momentarily, optimism differs because it is a *quality*. A quality that individuals possess, that allows them to overlook negativity. Optimism allows them to believe that some good can come from even a bad situation. Optimism is synonymous with expectancy.

I have had my own eyes opened to optimism recently, by a close friend who truly believes that all things happen for a reason. Even when it seems that our lives, and our relationships, do not turn out as planned there is always some good that comes out of it. If you have a job that you really despise, look at what you learned, and how that knowledge can help you advance to a better position. If you have been in a bad relationship, look at what it taught you, not only about your partner, but about yourself, and what you need to be looking for in future relationships. She pointed out to me that through my own experience, I have truly learned to appreciate others, and look less at my own needs. She taught me that to encourage others around me not only satisfies my own feelings of self-worth, but that by believing in, and encouraging others, I will find that others will in turn provide encouragement to me. This is true reciprocity. This is the silver lining. This is the beauty of being optimistic.

Optimism allows you to see both the good and bad in others and base your relationship on the positive things, while avoiding setting negative expectations based on minor flaws. After all, none of us is perfect. You just have to be accepting and more often than not, you will bring out the best in each other.

"Few things in the world are more powerful than a positive push. A smile. A world of optimism and hope. A "you can do it" when things are tough."

Richard M. DeVos

Persistent

"Refusing to give up or let go".

Having persistence is to refuse to allow obstacles, or emotions, to interfere with achievement or goals. We exhibit expectancy, as we do so many other qualities I have detailed in this book, in our work, in school, in athletics. Somehow, though, we seem to overlook persistence as a necessary quality to have in a relationship, at least until we lose control of a relationship, or feel it coming to an end. This is where I first recognized persistence to be as essential to relationships as it is in all other areas of our life.

It wasn't until the end of my two year separation that ultimately ended in divorce, do I believe that I demonstrated the highest level of persistence I ever had. Perhaps even more persistence than I had exhibited throughout the entire twenty years of my marriage. I did not want to let go. What I later came to realize, is that as persistent as I was in trying to win my wife back -- ironically when it was too late -- is how persistent I should have been throughout our marriage. To ensure that in my marriage, that goal of forever we set for our relationship, was achieved together. I didn't see how many obstacles, primarily those negative expectations I had, that I allowed to get in my way. I was not resolute in my efforts to see the marriage succeed.

"The art of love is largely the art of persistence."
Albert Ellis

After my marriage ended I realized the persistence I was demonstrating was more an effort to win back what

I had lost; a *new* goal. Not the goal I should have originally set at the start of the relationship. If we truly wish to succeed in our relationships, we need to state to each other clearly, in the beginning, what our goals are. "I will love you forever." is the most common declaration of a goal we make in the earliest stages of our relationship, when everything is new and wonderful. While this goal may appear to be expectancy, it is generally only another expectation.

Setting a goal for a lasting relationship, through expectancy, means that you must remain persistent, while recognizing that there will be ups and downs. This is the gold medal we should strive for in our relationship. Just as athletes persevere in their efforts to win by overcoming pain, injury, and other setbacks to achieve their goals, we should maintain the same level of persistence. To succeed by overcoming any obstacles that manifest as our relationship grows and changes.

Now is a good time to *S.T.O.P.* to return to the inventory you created earlier. Are you now able to see, and understand, where your own actions and reactions, your behavior, have in fact contributed to some of the failure of your relationship to thrive? If you can't find any fault in yourself, well I venture to guess you have stopped reading this book by now. If you can find fault in yourself, as well as in your partner, know that it may be possible to repair the damage before it is too late. If you don't truly love the person you are with, then it will be evident through the actions of yourself, and your partner, after your evaluation is complete. If you still choose to move out of the relationship, there is no real reason you cannot remain as the friends you once were, or should have been. You just need to be willing to apply some of what I've learned and shared with you. If you decide to move forward, or start over with a renewed purpose, then have a blast, because you may have just returned to Stage One – Growth -- the Romance Stage!

"Romance is everything."
Gertrude Stein

CHAPTER EIGHT

Keep the F.I.R.E. Burning

"The mind is not a vessel to be filled,

but a fire to be kindled."

Plutarch

- Chapter Eight -

So now we know that when we begin a new relationship, we often allow ourselves to succumb to the *Halo Effect,* that constant error. We tend to place, or visualize, a halo above our perfect partner, and our perceived perfect relationship. Searching only for "the perfect partner," however, skews our ability to see, to create, and to cultivate an ideal relationship. Frequently, we try to invent relationships based on unrealistic expectations that ultimately lead to failure. Perception of what our relationship is, or idealization of what we want our relationship to be, often creates a sense of tunnel vision. This, more often than not, will result in dissatisfaction and disillusionment once the cover is pulled back, to reveal what we, and our relationships truly are; a part of the human condition.

The dictionary defines the human condition as *"the positive and negative aspects of existence as a human being."* The halo effect, however, fails to take into account any negatives. My purpose in creating *Halo Again* is to help you to understand that relationships are discoveries, not inventions. That as much as when man first discovered fire, relationships are something that already exist in nature waiting to be revealed.

"The minute I heard my first love story, I started looking for you, not knowing how blind that was. Lovers don't finally meet somewhere. They're in each other all along."
Rumi

Each time we enter a relationship, that desire to be with *"the one"* overtakes our sensibilities. When we try to *invent* a future with that person based on the expectation that they are perfect, we tend to believe that the relationship will automatically be perfect, and will ultimately require no work. This creates a situation that often forces unwanted changes upon our self, or our partner, or ultimately ends. What we should do, is simply take the time to discover each other, and what our future can be together. This can only be accomplished through effective communication, not through pretenses and expectations, as I've stated many times before.

Relationships, like fire, can be a source of warmth and light but if not properly harnessed, like fire can quickly become destructive. While a fire can be appear to be extinguished, it only takes a little spark to reignite the flame. Communication then, in relationships, is the spark that ignites the flame. Positive messages keep the fire glowing, allowing you to sit back and enjoy the warmth, while negative messages are like throwing gasoline on a fire causing it to rage out of control.

Fire, in nature, is a chemical reaction that cannot be started without heat, fuel, and oxygen. Once started, fuel must be continually supplied to keep the fire burning. When we first meet, our passion -- our natural fuel -- is ignited by our energy and desire. If you do not continue to supply a fire with fuel, however, it will simply burn itself out. The same happens with relationships. When our relationships fail to receive adequate fuel, and begin to burn out, we call it complacency. When we are running low on fuel, our passion, it is because we are no longer communicating our needs and desires to each other. We assume that we know all we need to know about each other, and in believing this, we begin to lose our energy and desire.

When we stop talking to each other, stop exploring each other, stop remembering that change is inevitable and ongoing, we start taking the ones we love for granted. Believing that what is now, is all that will ever be in our relationship, we lose the spark. Those who love the warmth and coziness of a fireplace know that it requires a bit of work to keep it going all night. In most cases, flames gradually turn into embers. You must poke the firewood, and add more logs, as often as once an hour to keep a steady flame. To keep a relationship fire burning, you must be willing to put in the effort to maintain an adequate fuel supply. The elements of the fuel, your passion, that are needed to keep a relationship fire burning are _F_aith, _I_nterdependence, _R_esolve and _E_ssence. It is necessary, then, to understand each element from a communication standpoint.

"To succeed you have to believe in something with such a passion that it becomes a reality."
Anita Roddick

Faith

"Belief that is not based on proof."

My Roman Catholic roots have shown me often in my life, how important faith in God is in order to achieve salvation.   Faith transforms us.   Faith redefines and redirects us. Faith gives us purpose. Faith is not religion, faith is trust.   Faith is expectancy.   Having faith is to envision, and feel, that which is not ready to be seen or heard.   It is the confidence to accept, without question, that what we believe to be true is true. When we trust God completely, when we have faith in him, he will give us faith in our self, and in our partner.

Faith, then, is the primary element of the fuel that keeps the fire of any relationship burning. Faith keeps our hopes   and   dreams   alive.   It   creates   a   climate   of expectancy.   It   keeps   us   on   a   positive   path.   In   our relationships, just as with religion, faith provides us with the   strength   to   push   past   any   obstacle.   When   we   are strong in our faith, we can look at the trials that life throws our   way   with   objectivity,   allowing   us   to   understand ourselves, our partner, and to make wiser choices.   Faith also allows us to feel the needs of others, not just those of our own.

People   without   faith   are   those   who   often   live guided   only   by   reason   and   logic.   Logic,   much   like criticism,   tends   to   seek   solutions   by   reasoning, argumentation,   analysis,   and   ultimately   provides judgment.   While reason and logic do have a specific purpose in life, in relationships, those emotionally charged human   interactions,   we   need   faith   which   is   based primarily on trust. Both trust and faith are an acceptance without evidence or proof. We tend to use logic in our relationships as a self-serving tool to identify, and stress the mistakes of others, even setting expectations of failure. This, however, is the exact opposite of faith. Faith doesn't seek or stress any possible negatives.

"Faith consists of believing when it is beyond the power of reason to believe."
Voltaire

How, you ask, does faith have anything to do with the passion you experience when you first meet? That glowing feeling, that exuberance, that knowing that this person is *"the one"* and that you would do anything to keep this person happy. What else is that but faith? You have no proof, only a belief, and a desire to capture and keep this moment of happiness forever. Why, then, are we so quick to discard each other when the passion we first experienced is gone? It is because we didn't really have faith. What we were experiencing was lust, or an attempt to evade loneliness. Unfortunately, these expectations generally do end in failure.

True faith is the willingness to believe that the fire will never be extinguished as long as you put forth the extra effort to ensure that fire stays lit. In communication, this means you must acknowledge each other every day, for the little things you both do for each other. Avoid, at all costs, nagging which is an obvious indicator that your partner is not living up to some expectation you have set for them. If something isn't done, then do it! There is no reason to assume that any duties are the sole responsibility of only one of you. Look to your partner to see how you can better their day. The most important thing we forget is that to receive we must also give. If you find yourself coming home after a long day of work, and finding the house in disarray and no dinner cooked, it might just be the time to propose a night out. Especially if you find your partner is stressed, or was just too tired to deal with the mess that day. What this says to them is that you truly love them! Instead of the alternative, which is to come home, complain about what wasn't done, and start a fight. You will have indeed sparked a fire alright!

Never take your partner for granted. Your relationship is a gift, so treasure it, have faith in it, and build it for a lifetime…not a moment in time. Always have faith that the best is yet to come, and you will be opening the door to a wondrous future together. Life can be as exciting as when you first met if you say, and show each other love every day, in the smallest of ways. Express to each other often, how much you value your time together, and most importantly, as I stressed to you in the beginning of this book, treasure each moment of the life you have together.

"Life, if well lived, is long enough."
Lucius Annaeus Seneca

Interdependence

"Mutually reliant on each other".

One of the most beautiful aspects of any relationship is that we become a partnership working with each other, not independently of each other. This sharing is expectancy in its truest form. In a relationship based on interdependence, both partners share in the union, contribute to the union, and each gains benefit from the other, a symbiosis of sorts.

What most of us learned as children growing up, was that the wife was to be submissive, and the husband dominant. These traditional beliefs, and again I am not trying to disrespect the beliefs of others, are what set a lot of relationships up for failure today. These beliefs, these predetermined expectations, have become somewhat outdated in our society today because of the modern cultural differences that set us apart from a lot of other cultures. Those being our needs, and the right granted us, to be seen as unique individuals.

With this new understanding that relationships should be built on interdependence, versus dependence, it is undoubtedly those individual qualities that each of us possess that attract us to one another in the first place. How often have you heard the expression *"You make me a better person?"* That is exactly where interdependence comes into the relationship. This is saying that *"Until I met you, I never saw a reason for...,"* or, *"The beauty of..."* whatever it is that each of you contribute, that is now a part of what you share.

Interdependence in relationships is something we do not always recognize, even when it exists, therefore we fail to acknowledge the value this brings to the relationship. Still confused? Take two people, one who is extremely cynical, but funny and outgoing, and it is that humor that he or she possesses that brought them together – we'll call partner one the "comedian cynic." The other is sensitive and compassionate to everyone around them, but a bit reserved - let's call partner two the "compassionate sensitive." They meet, and there is an immediate chemistry between this seemingly, unlikely pair. The interdependence, that benefit that is gained here, is when the comedian cynic, if he/she truly loves the other, opens up to the sensitivity and compassion of the partner, and begins to understand, and integrate those traits into his or her own personality. While the compassionate sensitive gains a partner who has a more lighthearted attitude, and who can lift his/her spirits when life and issues become overwhelming.

The problem is we rarely look at ourselves as interdependent, as truly needing one another. We are too quick to discard our relationships when they "no longer work for us." If you do not acknowledge to your partner, as well as to yourself, those qualities that attracted you to each other in the first place, what you wind up with is two people unable to communicate. Two people who may ultimately grow tired of each other, which happens a lot more than it should. If you, the comedian cynic, did not appreciate the compassionate sensitive for those qualities he or she possessed, it is highly unlikely that you would have formed an attraction in the first place, and vice versa.

"In the progress of personality, first comes a declaration of independence, then a recognition of interdependence."
Henry Van Dyke

Tell each other what you love about each other; what you saw in the beginning, and still see in each other. Not *just* in the beginning of your relationship, but throughout, and more importantly often, and you will see an amazing light in your partner's eyes every time they look at you. It is that connection, that initial spark, that if you hold onto it dearly, will help you both weather the trials and struggles together. Let's face it, life itself ensures that we encounter struggles. There is no perfect relationship, but if you have assurance from your partner, together you can make it through anything. Discontentment and despair come in to play quickly when you begin to feel abandoned and alone, however it takes so little effort to keep this from happening. As I demonstrated earlier, even a simple nickel can change the direction of your life. Imagine an ocean of nickels just waiting to be discovered, if you seek them together.

It is also the misconception that marriage is a contractual arrangement, versus a union of interdependence that pervades our thoughts early in the relationship. The marriage contract has evolved in more recent times. I am not referring to the vows we take, but to the agreements we make that have been designed more or less, to secure provisions for either party if the contract is ever to be terminated. We enter our unions with these prenuptial agreements, that not only provide financial security in the event the marriage ends, but often in modern times go further to summarize each person's obligations to the other. These agreements do not serve to regulate how things are to work in the marriage, but rather how things will be settled when the union ends. This signifies to me, an expectation that there *will* be an end.

The same as with the investment strategy we use when determining whether a relationship has value to us, the marriage contract serves to take as fact what we feel about our partner, rather than allowing us to truly feel what we feel. To properly determine what someone's real value is to us is to allow ourselves to see and understand the benefit, the interdependence that we gain from them. To cherish those qualities that they possess: that captivate us, compliment us, and encourage us without words, to want to change ourselves. Contracts can be broken, but real love does not need to be contracted, nor can those bonds, if we never lose sight of why we formed them, ever be broken. We simply need to declare them.

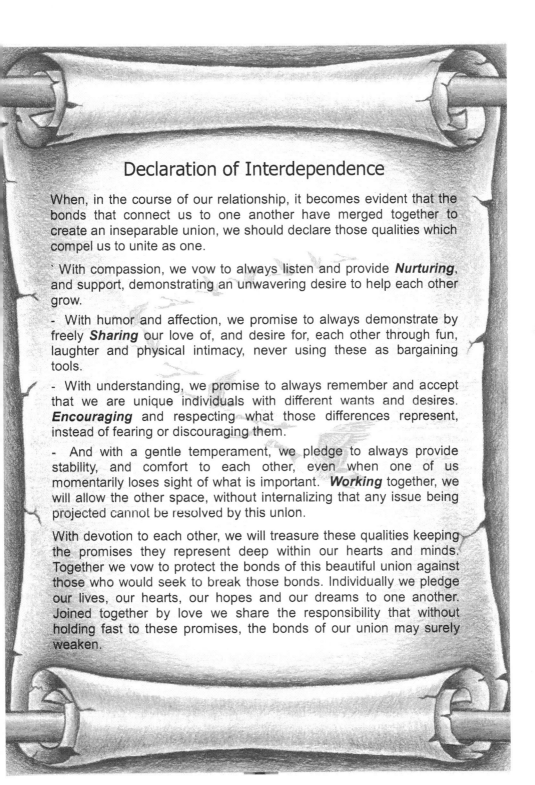

Declaration of Interdependence

When, in the course of our relationship, it becomes evident that the bonds that connect us to one another have merged together to create an inseparable union, we should declare those qualities which compel us to unite as one.

` With compassion, we vow to always listen and provide **Nurturing**, and support, demonstrating an unwavering desire to help each other grow.

- With humor and affection, we promise to always demonstrate by freely **Sharing** our love of, and desire for, each other through fun, laughter and physical intimacy, never using these as bargaining tools.

- With understanding, we promise to always remember and accept that we are unique individuals with different wants and desires. **Encouraging** and respecting what those differences represent, instead of fearing or discouraging them.

- And with a gentle temperament, we pledge to always provide stability, and comfort to each other, even when one of us momentarily loses sight of what is important. **Working** together, we will allow the other space, without internalizing that any issue being projected cannot be resolved by this union.

With devotion to each other, we will treasure these qualities keeping the promises they represent deep within our hearts and minds. Together we vow to protect the bonds of this beautiful union against those who would seek to break those bonds. Individually we pledge our lives, our hearts, our hopes and our dreams to one another. Joined together by love we share the responsibility that without holding fast to these promises, the bonds of our union may surely weaken.

Resolve

*"Firmness of purpose or
intent; determination."*

Healthy relationships are also based on the
determination that the two partners have in staying the
course with the long term investment, rather than seeking
a short term immediate return. Having a firm
determination, as well as a strong commitment, are the
characteristics of expectancy necessary to achieving
success in business, but in terms of relationships, we often
fail to incorporate these necessary qualities. When we
lack resolve we are usually unsuccessful in keeping the
fire lit.

The start of most relationships is based, primarily,
on the expectations we form based on that initial magic
we feel when we first meet. That desire for immediate
return on our investment. We often do not possess the
resolve, the determination, to stay the course once we feel
there is no more value in the investment. It is important to
understand that magic is only an illusion. It is an illusion
that we either perceive, or create. If we only perceive an
illusion to be real, when the veil of mystery is pulled away
to reveal the truth, we become disillusioned. When our
expectations are not met, we allow the fire to die slowly,
until eventually, it extinguishes itself completely. When
we work hard, on the other hand, to create magic, it is the
effort we put forth, the commitment and determination to
amaze our partner that demonstrates our desire, our
resolve, to keep the fire burning.

> **"Determination gives you the resolve to keep going in spite of the roadblocks that lay before you."**
> *Denis Waitley*

There are those who will tell you that relationships are work, and that you should carefully plan events, such as date night, or romantic dinners at home. I find there is little romance in planning. I find that spontaneity brings more to a relationship than planning! Even with the most carefully scheduled event, plans can change, or be disrupted leading to disappointment. In discovering how to maintain the fire, through creating little moments of magic, I saw where I failed. Acts of magic only last a moment, so we have to continue to believe in, and create magic, giving us the resolve to continually stoke the fire. If those first few feats fail to produce an immediate return, we are quick to pull out and reinvest with someone else, rather than to stay the course.

> **"You can give without loving, but you can never love without giving."**
> *Unknown*

You must remain determined to keep your relationship moving in a positive direction. To do so requires that you maintain a positive attitude. Don't let little moments of frustration turn into big storms that force you to change course from the direction you need to be heading. In life, as in business, it takes a positive attitude combined with *resolve* to achieve success. It takes exactly the same combination to achieve success in relationships.

Essence

*"A property of something without which
it would not exist or be what it is."*

In short, essence is meaning. Love and friendship give meaning to our lives, and combined, they are the foundation on which any relationship should be built. Love cannot exist without friendship, and friendship cannot exist without love. Just as we are interdependent on each other, these two states of our relationship are not only interdependent, but determine its success or failure.

While we all recognize that love and friendship give meaning to our lives, we fail to realize that it is us, as two unique individuals, and the traits we each possess that give meaning, give essence, to our love. It is this inner significance we bring to the union that we often fail to identify in our self or our partner. We allow it to become shelved or ignored, leading to the loss of meaning in our relationships. We are the essence of that love -- that last critical element of passion -- the fuel needed to keep the fire burning.

"Love in its essence is spiritual fire."
Lucius Annaeus Seneca

In philosophy, essence is defined to be the attributes that make something, or someone, what they fundamentally are, without which, they would lose their identity. This makes it necessary to recognize that if we lose faith, lose sight of those qualities that created our interdependence, and lose resolve, we have lost the essence by which our love was defined.

Too often, as in physics, we characterize or define something based on the absence or lack of its defined opposite. Darkness, for example, is defined as the absence of light, and does not in itself, actually exist. Similarly, cold is defined as the absence of heat. We need to identify the essence of our relationship, not what is absent. To see what defines the relationship, and to identify where we lack the measurable benefit that created meaning for us in the first place.

"Darkness cannot drive out darkness: only light can do that. Hate cannot drive out hate: only love can do that."
Martin Luther King, Jr.

CONCLUSION

"Your task is not to seek love, but to seek
and find all the barriers within yourself
that you have built against it."

Rumi

- Conclusion -

I see now just how unprepared I was at the time my wife and I began our journey together. My expectations were not fulfilled because my actions and reactions were inconsistent with my dreams and desires. While I had many expectations, I certainly lacked expectancy. Although I desired happiness, love, and an unwavering loyalty from my wife, it was our actions, inconsistent and often negative, that served to show us both the truth; that while two of us were in the marriage, neither of us was truly in the relationship.

I hope by now that you have learned that there needs to be romance in life, just as there is in love. This is why we have artists and poets in the world. They inspire us to inspire those closest to us. Nothing is more rewarding than to see the sparkle in the eye of someone you love every time you enter the room, no matter how long you've been together. That sparkle in the eye that I have observed in other relationships is pride. The idiom *"pride and joy"* is: someone or something that is cherished, valued, or enjoyed above all others. That sparkle is there because the one you love sees you as a treasure!

**"For where your treasure is,
there your heart will be also."**
Matthew 6:21

I have come full circle now. From now on, I vow to go forward looking to the future with renewed enthusiasm. The next time I fall in love it certainly won't be based on the expectation of beauty and perfection that the *halo error* represents. It will be based upon expectancy, and the belief that together we can overcome anything. With a view of life, that envisions and creates a foundation of hope for a caring and lasting future together. I shall use my eyes to see how gifted people are, my lips to encourage them to grow, my heart to help others realize how valuable they are, and I will hold out my hands to them to show them they are never alone. Above all else, I vow to keep open, honest communication with those I hold dearest to me. We must cherish every moment we have with those we love, because we may not have tomorrow. I will never again miss a conversation with those I love waiting for tomorrow, because tomorrow may just be too late.

What I believed before -- what has been stated by so many others -- is that love has no boundaries, that love is automatic, that love-at-first sight is true love, and that you must cross a finish line to reach love. But after you've won, what is left besides a trophy, a memory of a past achievement that tarnishes with age. Instead, what I've discovered is that no treasure was ever found without a compass to guide the journey, and that no journey should ever be taken without some direction, some ultimate destination. I've discovered that there are boundaries that serve as reference points to where the treasure lies buried. I have found that love is not always automatic, that you have to work to keep it alive. I have found that love-at-first sight is often just lust without friendship and faith to fuel the fire. I have found that love can grow from friendship, and that friendship must come first. I have found that friendship is the ultimate form of love, that it is not a race. Friendship and love never cross a finish line, they just continue to move forward.

True love and friendship are a reflection of our selves as individuals, as well as our united identity and destiny. You cannot put a halo over a person and expect the light it emanates to glow forever if all you do is cast dark shadows instead of reflections, and then run before the storm. The halo should never represent what we expect a person to be, it should be a representation of the treasure, the love we choose to share and grow. To be polished often by both, so that the light shining from it is never extinguished.

"Though we travel the world over to find the beautiful, we must carry it with us or we find it not."
Ralph Waldo Emerson

By writing this book, to close the last chapter of my life and start anew, I hope that I have shared some valuable insight that may help you sustain or restore the relationship you are in. Or, to help you on your own journey to find true love!

[END]

BIBLIOGRAPHY

Definitions: www.thefreedictionary.com

Downing, Skip. *On Course: Strategies for Creating Success in College and in Life.* Houghton Mifflin Company, 2008.

Frankl, Viktor. *Man's Search for Meaning.* Toronto lecture 1972.

Horton, R. S. (2003). Similarity and attractiveness in social perception: Differentiating between biases for the self and the beautiful. *Self and Identity, 2*, 137-152.

Kendrick, Alex, et al. *Fireproof: .* Culver City, Calif.: Sony Pictures Home Entertainment, 2009.

McNeish, Dr. Robert. *Lessons From the Geese.* Unpublished work. 1972.

Plutarch., John Langhorne, and William Langhorne. *Plutarch's Lives of Illustrious Men.* A new ed., with numerous portraits. London: Chatto & Windus, 1903. Print.

Thorndike, E.L (1). "A constant error in psychological ratings.". *Journal of Applied Psychology* **4** (1): 25–29.

Vroom, V. H. *Work and Motivation.* New York, NY: John Wiley and Sons, 1964.

RECOMMENDED READING

Albom, Mitch. *The Five People You Meet In Heaven*. New York: Hyperion, 2003.

Downing, Skip. *On Course: Strategies For Creating Success In College And In Life 6th Ed.*, Boston: Wadsworth Cengage Learning, 2011.

Harris, Joshua. *Boy Meets Girl*. Multnomah Books, 2000, 2005.

Osteen, Joel. *Your Best Life Now: 7 Steps to Living at Your Full Potential*. New York: Hachette Book Group USA, 2004.

Tolle, Eckhart. *A New Earth: Awakening to Your Life's Purpose*. New York: Penguin Group (USA) Inc., 2005.

Made in the USA
Charleston, SC
14 March 2014